THROUGH THE YEAR DEVOTIONALS

Courageous Faith
by Bill Hybels

Days of Grace
by Lewis B. Smedes

Hearing God
by Dallas Willard

Joy in the Journey
by Michael Card

Knowing God
by J. I. Packer

My Heart—Christ's Home
by Robert Boyd Munger and others

JOY IN THE JOURNEY

Through the Year

Michael Card

Compiled and Edited by Dale and Sandy Larsen

IVP Books

An imprint of InterVarsity Press
Downers Grove, Illinois

InterVarsity Press
P.O. Box 1400, Downers Grove, IL 60515-1426
World Wide Web: www.ivpress.com
E-mail: email@ivpress.com

InterVarsity Press® is the book-publishing division of InterVarsity Christian Fellowship/USA®, a student movement active on campus at hundreds of universities, colleges and schools of nursing in the United States of America, and a member movement of the International Fellowship of Evangelical Students. For information about local and regional activities, write Public Relations Dept., InterVarsity Christian Fellowship/USA, 6400 Schroeder Rd., P.O. Box 7895, Madison, WI 53707-7895, or visit the IVCF website at <www.intervarsity.org>.

Design: Cindy Kiple

Images: Eric Bean/Getty Images

ISBN 978-0-8308-3295-8

Printed in the United States of America ∞

Library of Congress Cataloging-in-Publication Data

Card, Michael, 1957-
    Joy in the journey through the year/Michael Card; compiled and
    edited by Dale and Sandy Larsen
      p; cm.—(Through the year devotionals)
    ISBN 978-0-8308-3295-8 (pbk.: alk. paper)
    1. Devotional literature. I. Larsen, Dale. II. Larsen, Sandy. III.
    Title.
    BV4811.C34 2007
    242'.2—dc22
                                        2007016687

P	20	·19	18	17	16	15	14	13	12	11	10	9	8	7	6	5	4	3	2	1
Y	24	23	22	21	20	19	18	17	16	15	14	13	12	11	10	, 09	08	07			

Joy in the Lord

> Come, let us sing for joy to the LORD;
>   let us shout aloud to the Rock of our salvation.
> Let us come before him with thanksgiving
>   and extol him with music and song.

PSALM 95:1-2

As you use this book, you will be continually confronted with God incarnate. This is the God who enters into our world and your individual life in the unique person of Jesus Christ. You will be reminded of how he walks with you daily. You will be led to take special notice of the ways he cares about you. You will be comforted to know that he weeps with you. Above all, you will be encouraged to see how he offers you his joy in all circumstances.

Each page gives a brief Scripture and accompanying devotional thoughts. At the bottom of each page is an activity which guides you to begin to respond to what you have read—to pray, to reflect or to make practical application in your life. The three suggestions will overlap as reflection leads to prayer, prayer motivates application, and application spurs further prayer and reflection.

You may feel led to write your thoughts and prayers in a journal. Especially if reflection raises questions for you, it can be helpful to jot down your thoughts on paper. Also some prayers are better written in a journal because you need to be more definite with your words. You can also look back more readily to see God's answers. Sometimes God will speak to you through reflection in a way that is so stunning that you must record it and read it again later.

You will find a year's worth of devotions here, designed to fill six days a week. We choose to offer six rather than seven days for a built-in bit of grace, as circumstances sometimes infringe on our devotional time. You can use the seventh day to go back to some of the *Pray, Journal* and *Apply* suggestions.

These devotions are not dated. You can start anywhere and move around as you please. There are devotions appropriate for Lent and Holy Week in weeks six through eleven. If you want devotions appropriate for Advent and Christmas, you will find them in weeks forty-seven through fifty-one.

These devotions are adapted from Michael Card's books *Immanuel, The Promise, A Fragile Stone, Scribbling in the Sand* and *Unveiled Hope,* along with other writings by Michael Card.

As you begin your journey through the year, talk to God about your motives for reading this book. Thank him that no matter what the circumstances of your journey, he offers you his joy. Let his joy continue to be your strength.

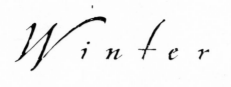

Winter

M O N D A Y

The Word We Call Jesus

In the beginning was the Word,
and the Word was with God, and the Word was God.

JOHN 1 : 1

For me, finding the right words for a lyric isn't as difficult as filling a page with prose. The structures of meter and rhyme have become comfortable to me. The boundaries set by a melody are like walls that protect the words. I have come to feel safe there. But to have *only* words!

Almost everyone knows what it's like to struggle with those clumsy bricks we call words, from Thomas Jefferson as he sought to define a new nation, to the student who tries to write about summer vacation. All our words are only stuttering and stammering in comparison to that one final, perfect Word, the Word of God.

In the history of the human struggle with words, most of them have been expended trying to define, outline, describe and articulate that obvious and elusive, simple and complex, childlike and mysterious Word. The Word that is God, the Word that became flesh, the Word that is Wisdom. The Word we call Jesus.

JOURNAL: *What comes to your mind when you think of the Word of God?*

TUESDAY

The Silence of the Heart

The Lord is in his holy temple;
let all the earth be silent before him.

HABAKKUK 2:20

I once experienced a crisis with words which was precipitated by an encounter with Silence. What came home to me powerfully was that silence really does say more than words. God speaks to us in the silence of the heart. Spoken or sung, words usually interfere with God's will as much as they help in seeing it done.

For a "vendor of words" like me, it was discouraging. When a new record was released that year it was disheartening to look at the blank bands between the songs on the L.P. and wonder if perhaps they contained more meaning than the grooves which contained the music and lyrics!

I am thankful that the Lord didn't leave me desolate in this crisis. He used the experience to give me a whole new appreciation both for words and for his Word. I was compelled to do my best to choose words with more care rather than to give up on them altogether.

PRAY: *When you pray, do you spend more time talking to God or listening to him? Pray that you will use this book to help you listen. Ask for more sensitivity to the Lord's voice. Then listen!*

WEDNESDAY

God Speaking to Us

For the kingdom of God is not a matter of talk but of power.

1 CORINTHIANS 4:20

To say that Jesus is the Word is another way of saying he is God speaking to us. While we struggle with our many clumsy words, God needs only one Word to perfectly communicate the depth and mystery, the passion and the overwhelming grace of who he is. By that Word, Light became a living being. Manna became man. Wisdom became a person. In him, Life came to life. All that God is came to us in that One Final Word we call Jesus.

My struggle to find words to describe him is at the same time a struggle to find him. My mind would like to believe that if I could only somehow put together the right combination of words, someday I would find him there at the end of them. But after all it is not a matter of words, as Paul says, but of power. The Power is Jesus himself.

APPLY: *When have you found that words fail you when you try to talk about Jesus? How have you experienced his power in ways you cannot put into words?*

"Who Do You Say I Am?"

Jesus . . . asked his disciples, "Who do people say the Son of Man is?"
They replied, "Some say John the Baptist; others say Elijah;
and still others, Jeremiah or one of the prophets."
"But what about you?" he asked. "Who do you say I am?"
Simon Peter answered, "You are the Christ, the Son of the living God."

MATTHEW 16:13-16

John has made it clear that Jesus does not need to ask people questions (John 2:24-25). Jesus is, in fact, offering the disciples an opportunity to confess who they believe him to be. He grants them an opportunity to take the next step in their faith and understanding of who he is.

Here, as in so many other places, Peter speaks for the Twelve. Had he not opened his mouth, the pain of the silence would have been unbearable. He does not directly answer the question as Jesus asked it. That is, he does not preface his statement with the words "We say you are . . ." Instead, he openly and forcefully confesses the fact, "You are the Christ, the Son of the living God."

JOURNAL: *What were the steps in your faith which led you to realize that Jesus is the Christ, the Son of the living God?*

Year~Round Christmas

My soul glorifies the Lord
and my spirit rejoices in God my Savior.

LUKE 1:46-47

The scenery of Christmas has become too familiar and comfortable. It blocks our view into the depth of the stark mystery of it all.

Perhaps the reason so many of us find it difficult to celebrate the birthday of Jesus is that we have confined the celebration to a single day, a day that's become more cluttered than any other day of the year, a day that better represents the noise and business of all our other days.

What if Christmas day were both a beginning and an end? The beginning of a celebration of Jesus that would not end until the next Christmas, when it would begin all over again?

What if the wise men's worship and the shepherds' awe became, if not a daily, then at least a weekly occurrence for us?

What if the peace and rest of the nativity became a part of every day?

What if Christmas were no longer a "holiday," but a *holy day*, infusing all our days with holiness?

JOURNAL: *No matter what day it is, today is a holy day. Christ has come to earth and is with you now. Consider ways you can celebrate his coming today and every day.*

Mysteries

> *"For my thoughts are not your thoughts,*
> *neither are your ways my ways,"*
> *declares the LORD.*

ISAIAH 55:8

I used to think that mysteries existed only to be solved. When I heard someone refer to the *mystery* of Christ, I assumed that Christ was a mystery only to nonbelievers. I have since learned that the mystery of Christ is reserved for those who do believe. To "know" the mystery of Christ is to realize that it is indeed just that, a mystery.

To represent faith in Jesus merely as something we come to understand and accept is to rob it of the mystery of being in relationship with something infinitely bigger and wiser than we are. His ways are not our ways, the prophet Isaiah tells us.

Mystery is not a category only for the spiritually elite, secret knowledge reserved for the members of the deeper life club. The mysteries of faith in Christ are for everyone who claims to be in relationship with him. The basic truths of Christianity are mysteries, not understandable, not "our ways": the virgin birth of Jesus, the Trinity, grace, prayer, the union of the believer with Christ, the cross, and perhaps most mysterious, and key to them all, the incarnation.

JOURNAL: *How is Christ still a mystery to you? How do you respond to the idea that you cannot fully comprehend Christ in this life—or perhaps ever?*

M O N D A Y

Your Servant Is Listening

> Then Eli realized that the LORD was calling the boy. So Eli told Samuel,
> "Go and lie down, and if he calls you, say, 'Speak, LORD, for your servant is listening.'"
>
> 1 SAMUEL 3:8-9

There is a lot of straight-out talk in the Law. But the apostle Paul points out that hearing it did not have much effect on fallen ears, beyond telling us, like a rigid schoolteacher, how hopeless we truly are. The rest of Scripture—the Prophets, the Psalms, the narratives of the Gospels, the visions of Revelation—speaks to the imagination, to that bridge inside us between heart and mind, that doorway to the soul. Imagination is what enables us to think with the heart and feel with the mind, a task Jesus seems intent on our learning to do.

That's why when God speaks it is so often in a vision, a parable, a metaphor or a song. These are ready vehicles for the imagination. The devotional life is nothing more or less than the process of listening to God through all the various means he has chosen to use: the Word, prayer, life. The source of our creativity is the overflow of the heart, the result of our devotional life.

APPLY: *To what extent do you allow the Lord to speak through your imagination? How can you better avail yourself of the visual arts, poetry, song and other creative means to let God speak to you?*

Writing a Lullaby

As he approached Jerusalem and saw the city, he wept over it.

LUKE 19:41

My response to the realization of the weeping baby Jesus was to write him a lullaby. For me it was a way of coming closer to his birth, to feel the darkness of that night, to smell the smells of the stable, and to hear the fragile newborn voice crying out in the night to his mother, Mary, and in a way, to me as well.

Since we know from Scripture that Jesus wept as a man, it is naive to think he did not cry as a baby. Tears are a basic part of what it means to be human. It is one of the sad signs of our fallen world that the first sign we give to show that we're alive is a cry. It was to this fallen world that Jesus came, not an imaginary one without tears. For the Man of Sorrows it would seem that tears were an even more integral part of his life than ours. He came as much to weep for us as to die for us.

JOURNAL: *What have you encountered lately that would make the Lord weep? How did your response to that situation compare with his response?*

The Child Grew

The child grew and became strong; he was filled with wisdom,
and the grace of God was upon him.

LUKE 2:40

By the time I was thirty I had been a Christian for twenty-two years. I was finished with college. I had been married to Susan for four years, and our first child, Katherine, had already come into the world. The ministry of teaching and music to which I had been called was well underway. I was basically *me*, the person I'll probably be until the day I die, for better or for worse.

In that story which is uniquely my story, the most important event had already taken place by the time I was eight years old. During a Sunday morning service I gave my life to Jesus and he gave his life to me. I struggle today to find the words to describe what happened. The best I can do is say I met him that day and realized that his extravagant demonstration of love on the cross was for me.

JOURNAL: *What part did Jesus play in your childhood? How have your ideas of him changed since then? Are there aspects of your childhood faith to which you would like to return?*

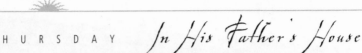

In His Father's House

"Why were you searching for me?" he asked.
"Didn't you know I had to be in my Father's house?"

LUKE 2:49

Jesus was only twelve. His parents always came to Jerusalem for the Feast of Passover. Whether they always took him along, we do not know. Nor do we know if the Passover meal had a particular impact on the young boy, if it made him weep or become thoughtful. The one thing we do know is that Jesus' parents lost him! Imagine being entrusted with raising the Messiah, only to lose him, not for a few moments but for three days!

When Mary and Joseph finally found Jesus, he was in the temple. He was with the teachers, the same group he would come into conflict with so often as a man. Was he dumbfounding them with his wisdom? Was he asking simple but unanswerable questions to confound them? Luke tells us only that those who heard were "amazed at his understanding and his answers."

While the teachers were amazed, Joseph and Mary were astonished. But Jesus could not understand why they would have looked anywhere else but in the temple, his Father's house.

JOURNAL: *Imagine yourself as one of the teachers who listened to the twelve-year-old Jesus in the temple. What do you think of him? How do you respond to him?*

A Most Unlikely Boy

After three days they found him in the temple courts,
sitting among the teachers, listening to them and asking them questions.

LUKE 2:46

I've always imagined an elderly rabbi who was just curious enough to stay and listen to the young Jesus. Convicted by his words, the teacher does not stay for long. Later that night he realizes the voice of God was indeed speaking through that most unlikely Galilean boy. Early the next morning he runs back to the temple to look for Jesus, only to find that his parents have already come and taken him home.

I suppose the old rabbi of my imagination is really me. I would have been the one who stood in the back of the crowd and listened only as long as my busy schedule allowed. I would have made an immediate judgment on the boy: "He's too young. What does he know?" His poor circumstances would have made me certain that he had nothing of value to say.

I trust that the Lord would have broken through the wall of my foolishness, as he does today. Though I'll never know for sure, I pray that I would have come running back to find that young boy who spoke the words of God.

PRAY: *In Christ is all wisdom. Bring your biggest questions to Jesus and trust him for the answers.*

The Son's Obedience

*As Jesus was coming up out of the water, he saw heaven being torn open
and the Spirit descending on him like a dove. And a voice came from heaven:
"You are my Son, whom I love; with you I am well pleased."*

MARK 1:10-11

Children are constantly being called on to do things they don't understand.
My mother said, "Wash up," but I knew I'd be dirty again in five minutes. My
father said, "Mow the lawn," but it would only grow back by next week. My
daughter is in pain with an infection and I ask her to be still while a doctor
painfully sticks a long needle into her flesh.

God said to his Son, "Get in the water!" And without protesting, Jesus
obeyed. "I am well pleased, my Son," the Father responded. You can almost
feel the Father's pure pride. God said, "Drink this cup of suffering," and Jesus,
who had openly confessed that he didn't want to do it, said, "Yet not as I will,
but as you will." From that same radical obedience—an obedience that submits even to what may seem senseless, that does not demand to see the meaning of it all—from that obedience came the salvation of the world.

APPLY: *How is God calling you to obey in some way you don't understand? If you
are sure it's his voice, trust him and go ahead and obey.*

MONDAY *The Face of Jesus*

> *For God, who said, "Let light shine out of darkness,"*
> *made his light shine in our hearts to give us the light of the*
> *knowledge of the glory of God in the face of Christ.*

2 CORINTHIANS 4:6

All of my life I have had a deep yearning to see the face of Jesus, to know what he looks like. I have resorted to seeking out his image on the faces of his children. From time to time I catch a glimpse of a smile that must be like his, or I see someone express compassion as he would.

To this day when someone boasts of having a vision of him, inwardly I burn with jealousy. I wonder sometimes why seeing him hasn't resulted in a more profound change in the person's life. Then I stop and realize that I would probably be no different. I trust that he knows what he is doing, hiding himself from me among his children. Still I hope that someday someone will see something of his face in mine.

PRAY: *Pray that you will see the face of Jesus in others, and that others will see the face of Jesus in you.*

The Visible Christ

For you died, and your life is now hidden with Christ in God.
When Christ, who is your life, appears, then you also will appear with him in glory.

COLOSSIANS 3:3-4

A group from our church was visiting a rescue mission when something miraculous happened to me. One of the group was spending time with an elderly man who bore all the classic signs of the street alcoholic. The Lord spoke to me in a way I had never experienced. As I watched our team member open himself to this man, he disappeared and Christ became visible. And as the alcoholic man received the lovingkindness of my friend, he too began to disappear and take on the image of Christ, who was present in his pain and need.

I am not saying Christ was living in this man simply because he was poor. Perhaps Jesus was present in the reaching out of both of them. I don't pretend to understand all that happened in that moment. Yet it was clear that the two were no longer visible. Paul would have said that both of them were hidden in Christ.

JOURNAL: *When have you been suddenly and unexpectedly aware of the presence of Christ? What effect did the experience have on you?*

He Became Like Us

> *We know that when he appears, we shall be like him,*
> *for we shall see him as he is.*

1 J O H N 3 : 2

Julius Caesar boasted, "I came, I saw, I conquered." His empire crumbled, and he who was the conqueror became the conquered.

Jesus Christ, who possessed infinitely greater power, lived by an unexpected twist of Caesar's saying. Jesus lived by the motto, "I came, I saw, I surrendered."

Jesus' primary surrender was the taking on of human flesh, the incarnation. His surrender made possible the cross. Although he might have grasped equality with God, he surrendered to becoming human out of obedience to the Father. His human life began as it would end, based on the paradox of victory through surrender.

Jesus' total embrace of humanity, his becoming like us, is the basis of our hope to someday be like him. His identification with our frailty provides our confidence that someday we will cast aside our fragile, fallen humanity and see him as he is.

PRAY: *Do you value strength and power over frailty and surrender? Ask the Lord for a renewed vision of what Jesus gave up to become a human being and give his life for you.*

> When Jesus saw him lying there and learned that he had been
> in this condition for a long time, he asked him, "Do you want to get well?"

JOHN 5:6

Jesus had wonderful gifts to give: miracles, bread, wine, healing. His gifts were the main reason the crowds hounded him. Patiently, sometimes reluctantly, he doled out his gifts to thousands. But if you look more closely at his life and listen to the Gospels, you see that there was more he wanted to give.

Jesus encountered a man who had lounged beside the pool of Bethesda for thirty-eight years, pitifully clinging to his most treasured possession, his illness. Despite the man's whining, his lack of courage to become well and his faithlessness, Jesus uttered the command, "Get up." The man got up, picked up his mat and walked away, not even learning the name of the One who healed him.

Later Jesus went looking for the man and discovered him in the temple area. "Stop sinning or something worse will happen to you," Jesus said.

Something worse? Yes, something infinitely worse: meeting Jesus and not coming to really know him.

PRAY: *Thank the Lord for his material gifts, but ask him to continually help you to value him most. Embrace his gift of himself for you.*

Embrace the Giver

Thanks be to God for his indescribable gift!

2 CORINTHIANS 9:15

One Christmas my wife gave me a book I had wanted for a long time. It was a rather obscure book on N. C. Wyeth. When I discovered it (she had tried to hide it in the wardrobe) I was surprised and so happy. I didn't hug the book, however, and give it a big sloppy kiss. No, I dropped the book and embraced her, the one who had given such a special gift. As wonderful as the present was, it was she, Susan, who had gone to the trouble of special ordering it.

We reserve our thanksgiving and embraces for our loved ones, not the gifts they give. The same holds true in our relationship with that greatest of Givers. The temptation to foolishly embrace his gifts is greater because they are infinitely better and more beautiful.

JOURNAL: *Write about various gifts the Lord has given you, whether material things, honors, abilities or relationships. Then write about how the Lord himself is greater than each of them.*

It All Belongs to Him

Whom have I in heaven but you?
And earth has nothing I desire besides you.

PSALM 73:25

The "stars that do shine" and the rest of creation around us have all been embraced by different groups as idols to worship. After all, they are beautiful gifts from God. But their beauty is only a shadow of his beauty. If embracing them gives a certain joy, how much more joy would come from embracing him!

Perhaps we are tempted to embrace God's gifts because we really desire to possess them. But even the gift of life, something all of us cling to with both hands, cannot be possessed. God gives us fantastic gifts, but he wants us to remember that everything belongs to him. He wants to be our only possession.

APPLY: *What part of material creation holds too much power over you or takes up too much space in your affection? How will you surrender it to the Lord?*

M O N D A Y *A Lonely Messiah*

Jesus often withdrew to lonely places and prayed.

LUKE 5:16

I have always struggled with loneliness. At those times I often think about Jesus. All four Gospels talk about his loneliness and preference for lonely places. You can sense it between the lines of many of those passages, a holy melancholy. A lonely Messiah.

Jesus' disciples, whom he loves with much tenderness, often misunderstand him. They question. They doubt. They constantly miss whatever point he tries to make. When Jesus' family, believing him to be out of his mind, come to take charge of him, his response has a dull and lonely sound: "Who are my mother and my brothers?" When John the Baptist is murdered, Jesus' response is to retreat by himself. When the crowd tries to force him to become king, Jesus flees to the wilderness. I can almost see him wandering there, talking to himself and his Father, the only One who really understood.

When Jesus felt alone, it was because his Father was so visibly absent in the world. Jesus sought his Father's presence in lonely places. I wonder if their hearts resonated together with loneliness . . . for each other.

PRAY: *Talk to your Father about any ways in which you feel misunderstood or abandoned.*

Alone with the Father

A time is coming, and has come, when you will be scattered, each to his own home.
You will leave me all alone. Yet I am not alone, for my Father is with me.

JOHN 16:32

The Gospels tell us that when Jesus retreated to lonely places, it was for prayer. In his actions we can see a purpose in loneliness, both for Jesus and for us. The sense of aloneness forced Jesus to flee to a lonely place, to pray, to pour out his heart to the Father. One great conclusion is at the heart of Jesus' remedy for loneliness: If God, the Father of Jesus, really does exist, then none of us is alone, and indeed can never be.

Every time we let loneliness take over our feelings, we have lost sight of that personal, caring and loving Father. He is *Abba*, our Papa. Even if no other person understands or cares, he does. That is the God Jesus fled to when he felt lonely. The same caring Father is there for us.

APPLY: *In times of loneliness, whether prolonged or only for a moment, consciously turn to Christ and welcome his presence with you. Thank him for always being with you.*

Do not be quick with your mouth,
do not be hasty in your heart
to utter anything before God.
God is in heaven
and you are on earth,
so let your words be few.

ECCLESIASTES 5:2

The best way to show someone you love them is to listen to them," my friend Bill Lane told me once, on an unforgettable walk we took around campus where he was a professor and I was a student. I was agonizing over my future wife, who at that point gave me little or no reason to hope that my affections would ever be returned. Out of my own impatience, I was preparing for a showdown with her, a confrontation that would surely have destroyed what little relationship we had.

"If you really want to show her you love her," Bill said with characteristic intensity, "listen to her." I took his advice, and that girl has been my wife for over twenty years.

Later I extended my understanding of Bill's advice to my relationship with the Lord when I began to realize how much I wanted to show him the extent of my love for him. If we desire to demonstrate our love for God, shouldn't we invest in listening to him? Doesn't he demonstrate his love for us by listening endlessly to our prayers?

PRAY: *Spend time listening to God before you say anything to him in prayer.*

Listen to Him!

Then a cloud appeared and enveloped them, and a voice came from the cloud:
"This is my Son, whom I love. Listen to him!"

MARK 9:7

It may seem like an oversimplification, but basic to the art of listening is allowing the other person to speak, providing an open place in the conversation where they are granted the time, the space and the freedom to speak. As simple as this may sound, it can be a major task.

The same is true when it comes to allowing the Bible to speak for itself. We are to listen with as few presuppositions as possible, coming to the Word with the same sort of openness we might offer a friend who has let us know they have something important to tell us. In fact, the Bible does have something important to tell us, if we will have the grace and wisdom to hear it.

APPLY: *Go back to some passages of Scripture with which you are very familiar. Read them again, slowly, asking the Lord to give you new insight, even if it challenges your preconceived ideas.*

Listen to the Word

For the word of God is living and active. Sharper than any double-edged sword,
it penetrates even to dividing soul and spirit, joints and marrow;
it judges the thoughts and attitudes of the heart.

HEBREWS 4:12

When we try to listen to someone whose speech is slow or deliberate, the great temptation is to finish their sentences for them. The same is often true when we listen to God's Word, particularly to those passages with which we think we are familiar. But one of the great proofs that Scripture is alive is its ability to speak afresh through passages I thought I knew by heart. In fact I might have known them by "head," but not until they came alive in the heart have I really begun to listen.

A listening stance before the Word means keeping your mind as quiet as possible and letting the Bible finish its sentences, its stories. The simple act (which is sometimes not so simple) of quieting the mind and heart, and allowing the Bible to speak as if it had never spoken in its own voice to you before, will transform your time with the Word. Be quiet, be patient, and let it say what it has to say!

JOURNAL: *Read a passage of Scripture which is very familiar to you. Ask the Lord to show you something you have never noticed before or some new insight from that Scripture; then read the passage at least twice more, slowly. Make notes of new ideas or applications you receive from the Scripture passage.*

Reading Out Loud

Let anyone with ears to hear listen!

MARK 4:23 NRSV

Therefore consider carefully how you listen.

LUKE 8:18

In the ancient world all reading was done out loud. Even when one was alone, reading was done audibly. That is how Philip knew what section of the Old Testament the Ethiopian eunuch was reading in Acts 8.

Start reading Scripture out loud to yourself. Hearing the sound of your own voice speaking the words of Scripture can have a stunning effect. Passages we thought we knew by heart speak to us in a new way. Stories come alive with the wealth of detail Scripture provides. All at once the text takes on a new dimension of tone. We begin to hear a voice. We have begun to listen with the ears of our imagination.

APPLY: *Read a passage from the Bible aloud. If you are self-conscious, find a place where no one can hear you. As you read, vary the volume. Vary the speed, reading first rapidly, then slowly. Experiment with different tones of voice.*

M O N D A Y *Walls of Protection*

> *"And I myself will be a wall of fire around it,"*
> *declares the LORD, "and I will be its glory within."*

ZECHARIAH 2:5

We talk about breaking down walls between races, between sexes and so on. We don't talk enough about building walls to protect our brothers and sisters, walls to redemptively keep out negative aspects of the world. We need protective walls, which is to say we need community, which is to say (according to Zechariah) that we need God.

Jesus created at least three communities. First there were the twelve disciples, who were given authority to spread the good news. A second, more intimate level of community existed between Jesus and the three closest to him: Peter, James and John. A third level of community was the little-mentioned "seventy." This larger group of disciples was responsible for paving the way before Jesus arrived into a given area.

Community was a sustaining force to Jesus' person and ministry. And it provided the foundation for the church universal that he would build.

JOURNAL: *To what communities do you belong, either formally or informally? How does each one aid your spiritual growth?*

Good Counsel

*Perfume and incense bring joy to the heart,
and the pleasantness of one's friend springs from his earnest counsel.*

PROVERBS 27:9

My best friend Scott came by to see me. Because he is a pastor, his day is unbelievably busy. Nevertheless he sat down beside the fire and asked me where I was on a book manuscript. He listened to new ideas I was excited about. Above all, in the midst of what is always a painful, doubt-filled process, he encouraged me. He came because he knew I needed to hear someone say I could do this.

Twenty-five years earlier, I did something like that for Scott. He was frustrated writing and recording music and being on the road away from his growing family. Everywhere we went, Scott could always connect at a deep level, comforting and encouraging people.

That evening in the church parking lot, I said something like, "So many people can do the music; so few have the gifts you have. You are a pastor." He gave a deep sigh. He had been waiting for years to have someone confirm what he knew in his heart was true about himself.

PRAY: *Pray for your friends. Thank God for the ways in which they have helped you follow him more faithfully.*

Friends Define Each Other

You are my friends if you do what I command.
I no longer call you servants, because a servant does not know his master's business.
Instead, I have called you friends, for everything that I learned from my Father
I have made known to you.

JOHN 15:14-15

Friends help each other understand who the other is. They define one another over the course of a lifetime. When I am uncertain about the direction of my life, I go to my closest friends to affirm, or perhaps reaffirm, who I am and what the calling on my life is about.

If Jesus had a best friend, it was certainly Simon Peter. Certainly Jesus does not need to be told who he is. But perhaps in his humanity there was still from time to time the hunger for the assurance of his friend. And beyond a doubt Peter needed the defining presence of Jesus in his life, as we all do.

JOURNAL: *How does Jesus define you? How has the course of your friendship progressed?*

An Unlikely Team

Our dear friend Luke, the doctor, and Demas send greetings.

COLOSSIANS 4:14

Just after he arrived at Troas, before he left for Macedonia, Paul added to his team a thoughtful, bookish Gentile. The newcomer was a physician, a profession that in the first century was relegated almost solely to slaves or freedmen. As Paul and the Gentile set out on their first missionary journey together, they could never have guessed how deep their friendship would become. The newcomer bore a common slave-name. He was simply known as Luke.

Paul and Luke were an unlikely team. Could it be that Paul simply needed a doctor to travel with him to help treat whatever his "thorn in the flesh" might have been? Was it their mutual respect and concern for the marginal men and women of their time that brought Luke and Paul together in ministry? Or was it the fact that they both cared so deeply for the universality of the gospel that their hearts resonated with compassion for the Gentiles?

Perhaps it was for all those reasons and others. Paul and Luke were the sort of unlikely combination Jesus would use to change the world.

JOURNAL: *When has the Lord put you in an unlikely combination with another person or group of people for ministry? How were you changed through the experience?*

Faithful to the End

Only Luke is with me.

2 TIMOTHY 4:11

In his letter to Philemon, Paul refers to Luke as one of his fellow workers (Philemon 23). By the time he writes the letter to the Colossians he mentions Luke again, but now Paul singles him out as "our dear friend" (Colossians 4:14). By the end of his life Paul will say "only Luke is with me." Luke had become his most faithful friend. Who is to say that he did not stay at Paul's side until the very end, perhaps claiming and caring for the apostle's decapitated body?

APPLY: *Who are the people who have remained your most faithful friends? Take time to thank God for each of them. Consider the people—perhaps only one person—to whom you will remain faithful until the very end. Ask God for the grace to keep your commitment of friendship.*

A Woman of Hospitality

Simon's mother-in-law was suffering from a high fever, and they asked Jesus to help her.
So he bent over her and rebuked the fever, and it left her.
She got up at once and began to wait on them.

LUKE 4:38-39

Luke tells us that Jesus rebuked the fever. He spoke directly to it, telling it to leave. There is no recovery time, no word of Jesus telling someone to bring her something to eat as he later does with the little girl he raises. No, immediately she gets up and does for Jesus what she no doubt did for every visitor to that home. She served them the special evening Sabbath meal.

Her immediate and selfless servanthood speaks clearly of the tone she would have set in the home. It hints to us as well about what kind of woman Peter had taken as his bride—of the imprint of the mother on the daughter who became the wife. Apparently Peter's house was a home where hospitality was practiced, not because it was dictated by the culture, but because it came freely and easily to the two women of the house, the mother and the daughter.

APPLY: *Are there ways in which you can expand the hospitality of your home to further your personal ministry?*

M O N D A Y

A Senseless Dispute

> *A dispute arose among them as to which of them*
> *was considered to be greatest.*

LUKE 22:24

All along the way during that final journey to Jerusalem they had argued about it: who was the greatest? Some of the disciples described the material wealth they had left behind. Others loudly mentioned their superior preaching ability. Others ironically boasted that their humility was the greatest among the twelve.

Jesus had so longed to spend this time with them before he entered into his suffering. It was their last meal, their last chance to be together, and they were wasting it in the most colossal way.

Finally he had had enough. He did not lose his temper; he was too tired, too emotionally spent and too sad for that. Instead, without saying a word, he got up from the table. He had reached the point where he had given up on words. In his exhaustion he simply wanted to love them as best he could.

PRAY: *Where are you tempted to think of yourself as the greatest, the most capable, the most spiritual? Confess your pride to the Lord and accept his forgiveness.*

The Lord's Example

Now that I, your Lord and Teacher, have washed your feet,
you also should wash one another's feet.
I have set you an example that you should do as I have done for you.

JOHN 13:14-15

Jesus took off his long outer coat, leaving only the seamless robe that the soldiers would be gambling for in a few hours. He took a towel and wrapped it around his waist, then picked up the bowl of water that had been provided for washing their hands. By this time the twelve were silent. They looked on, wondering what he was up to. Jesus' intensity told them not to interrupt by asking to help.

He began with Thaddeus, then Andrew, Philip, James, Matthew. By the time he got to Thomas there were tears in his eyes. James, Matthew's brother, was next, then John; then, amazingly, Judas. Finally Jesus came to Simon Peter, whose voice had been the loudest in the argument about who was the greatest. Peter broke down and wept like a little boy. It was embarrassing to everyone except Jesus, who had waited so long to finally see him break.

They never argued again about who was the greatest.

JOURNAL: *Put yourself in the room of the Last Supper. Jesus approaches you to wash your feet. How do you feel? What do you say?*

"No," said Peter, "you shall never wash my feet."
Jesus answered, "Unless I wash you, you have no part in me."
"Then, Lord," Simon Peter replied, "not just my feet but my hands and my head as well!"

JOHN 13 : 8 - 9

Perhaps Peter's tone here is surly, taking into account his difficult and disappointing day. Simon, we recall, is the only one of the disciples who ever says "no" to Jesus. At this moment it is not a rejection of Jesus' friendship. It is a denial of who he really is: their Servant Lord. In essence, Peter is saying to Jesus, "You just don't get it, do you? This is not appropriate. Of all the inappropriate things that you've done, this is the most inappropriate."

John the Baptist alluded to the same dilemma when Jesus asked to be baptized by him. "This is not appropriate. You should be baptizing me." Jesus embraces sinners, and the Pharisees say, "What you're doing is not appropriate." He reaches out to prostitutes, he touches lepers, he touches the dead, and everyone says, "This is not appropriate."

JOURNAL: *Of all the events in Jesus' life which you read about in the Gospels, which is the most startling to you? Why does it strike you that way? What does it say to you about the Lord?*

The Servant Savior

He came to Simon Peter, who said to him, "Lord, are you going to wash my feet?"
Jesus replied, "You do not realize now what I am doing, but later you will understand."

JOHN 13:6-7

Peter was right. It was inappropriate for Jesus to be doing what he was doing. In Peter's and everyone else's mind the Messiah would never suffer, never submit, never serve. By the end of this long day Jesus will have done all three. And Peter will be bitterly disappointed with him. Jesus will fail to meet his expectations as the Christ, and perhaps even, that evening, as his friend. The world Peter has built around Jesus has begun to slowly fall apart. He has fallen victim to one of the great paradoxes of life as described by Kierkegaard: "Life must be lived forward but it can only be understood backwards."

Jesus' point is that if Peter denies the humility of his Servant Savior, he cannot possibly take part in what Jesus is doing. Until Peter submits to who Jesus really is, how can he become one of his disciples? For that matter, how can we?

APPLY: *If Jesus is the Servant Savior, what are the implications for your life as one of his followers?*

FRIDAY

Not to Be Served But to Serve

Whoever wants to become great among you must be your servant,
and whoever wants to be first must be slave of all.
For even the Son of Man did not come to be served, but to serve,
and to give his life as a ransom for many.

MARK 10:43-45

Jesus rises, still hungry, from his own supper and demonstrates what true greatness is. In the upside-down kingdom, true greatness is found in the servant's kneeling with the basin and the towel.

This vision of Jesus as Servant Savior provides a foundation for a biblical value system. What is more valuable, to be served or to serve? Though Peter protests, Jesus is insistent that unless Peter is willing to submit in humility to the servant lordship of Jesus, unless he is willing to obediently allow Jesus to wash his feet, he has nothing to do with what Jesus is doing.

Jesus longs to wash our feet, too, with the water of his Word, every day. He is serving us now, preparing a place for us in his Father's house, interceding for us before the Father. He promises to wait the table of the wedding supper of the Lamb—still the servant, still the same yesterday, today and forever.

APPLY: *Are there people the Lord is calling you to serve in a setting the world would consider unglamorous and unappealing? How will you respond to his call?*

The Servant Artist

For you were called to freedom, brothers and sisters;
only do not use your freedom as an opportunity for self-indulgence,
but through love become slaves to one another.

GALATIANS 5:13 NRSV

Whatever you do, don't react like Peter did and say no to the One who longs to approach you and me and tenderly give us the washing we so badly need. That is simply pride, the kind of pride that gets you into arguments about who is the greatest. For we will never be able to pick up the basin and towel, or the paintbrush or the ballet slipper, until we have first submitted in humility to the Servant Lord.

The call to servanthood causes the creative gift to come alive. It gives color and tone and direction and purpose. The art that naturally flows out of our obedient response to the call of God on our lives can, by grace, become water to wash the feet of sisters and brothers, cold water to quench the thirst of an unbelieving world. To become servants of Christ is the highest goal we can aspire to in our creative work.

PRAY: *Ask the Lord to give you a heart of service as he uses your gifts for ministry.*

MONDAY *The Place of Crushing*

> *Going a little farther, he fell to the ground and prayed*
> *that if possible the hour might pass from him.*
> *"Abba, Father," he said, "everything is possible for you. Take this cup from me.*
> *Yet not what I will, but what you will."*

MARK 14:35-36

Gethsemane literally means "place of crushing," a place where olives were crushed for their oil. That name took on an infinitely deeper meaning when Jesus knelt down there to pray that night in the garden.

A man knelt there, a man of unspeakable courage and obedience. Jesus looked the Father in the face with mature, though anguished, honesty and said, "If there is any way for this cup to pass, let it be so!" Yet a child also knelt down there to pray. "Abba, anything is possible for you!" Jesus' words sound like a child's cry to his father for help, not a theological statement about an all-powerful Universal Being.

Jesus cried out, "Abba." Never let anyone clothe that word in theological sophistication. It is not a sophisticated word. It is baby talk! *Papa, Daddy, Abba*—they are all the same thing: the first stutterings of an infant, not to be categorized in some theological structure, but to be cried out from the heart of a child, a heart of faith.

PRAY: *Bring the deepest cries of your heart to your Abba, your heavenly Father. Do not be ashamed of your feelings before him.*

Jesus . . . offered up prayers and petitions with loud cries and tears to the one
who could save him from death, and he was heard because of his reverent submission.

H E B R E W S   5 : 7 - 8

Long ago, in a garden, a great battle was lost when Adam responded to the call of God with the notion, "Not thy will, but mine be done." In another, darker garden called Gethsemane, we see Jesus struggling with his own will over against the will of the Father. Jesus comes into the battle saying, "If there is any way this cup can pass, if there is any way you can get me out of this, do it!" Knowing everything that lurks in the darkness before him, Jesus in his humanity says, "This is not what I want." What else does "nevertheless not my will but thine be done" mean if there was not a genuine conflict between two wills, Jesus' will and the Father's will, there in the garden?

The first seed of the victory won on the cross of Christ was sown in the garden. That seed was the radical obedience of the Son. The term *radical obedience* implies not doing what you want to do but doing the last thing in the world you want to do!

J O U R N A L : *What does radical obedience mean to you? When have you obeyed in that way? Who do you know that has obeyed in that way?*

Stay Awake and Pray

*Then he returned to his disciples and found them sleeping.
"Simon," he said to Peter, "are you asleep? Could you not keep watch for one hour?
Watch and pray so that you will not fall into temptation.
The spirit is willing, but the body is weak."*

MARK 14:37-38

Though Peter, James and John are all sound asleep, it is only Simon whom Jesus castigates. Earlier Peter had sworn he would follow Jesus to prison and even to death. Now he could not find it in himself to stay awake to watch with his agonizing Friend. Jesus, in the midst of his suffering, returns to make sure they are not falling into temptation. He had been praying for Peter. Now he instructs Peter to pray for himself.

The story of the Garden of Gethsemane is a story of the importance of prayer. Without the prayers of Jesus, we would not know his salvation. When Jesus said that the spirit is willing but the flesh is weak, I wonder if he was referring to both his own and the disciples' struggles.

JOURNAL: *Where is your flesh weak although your spirit is willing?*

Prayer Makes It Possible

He went away a second time and prayed,
"My Father, if it is not possible for this cup to be taken away unless I drink it,
may your will be done."

MATTHEW 26:42

If Jesus had ultimately refused the cup, the Father would have taken it away. And in that moment we would all have been lost. Yet the Son is able to choke out the words "I want your will not mine." For this moment he does not want the cup he is being offered. But if it is the Father's will, he will drink it to the dregs. If James and John were still awake at this point, I wonder if they understood the reference to the cup they themselves had said they were ready to drink (Mark 10:38-40).

Genuine obedience is not doing something we already want to do, but submitting to the last thing in the world we would do. The prayerful obedience of Jesus in the garden made possible the cross. Prayer makes everything possible.

PRAY: *Thank the Lord that he submitted to the Father. Pray for courage to obey even when obedience is difficult.*

A Familiar Face

Going at once to Jesus, Judas said, "Greetings, Rabbi!" and kissed him.
Jesus replied, "Friend, do what you came for."

MATTHEW 26:49-50

The Gospel writers avoided looking too closely at Judas. What's the use of looking at a man whose destiny was destruction? His was the face of death. Who wants to look at a face like that?

But there could be another reason why no one likes looking at Judas. Do we avoid him because we fear that we might see someone familiar when we look in his tormented eyes? Ourselves, perhaps? Is that why we like to specu- late that he was really manipulated by God into doing what he did? Wouldn't we really like to give ourselves the benefit of the doubt and blame God for our wrongdoing?

Look hard at Judas the next time you are tempted to manipulate people to get your own way. See if you don't recognize yourself. Then look again to the One who was betrayed. Know that he isn't looking at you the same way you're looking at yourself. Though we have all betrayed him, he is ready to welcome us and call us "friend."

APPLY: *In what ways have you betrayed or abandoned Jesus? How do you re- spond to the fact that he still calls you friend?*

Strangely In Charge

Jesus, knowing all that was going to happen to him, went out and asked them,
"Who is it you want?"
"Jesus of Nazareth," they replied.
"I am he," Jesus said. (And Judas the traitor was standing there with them.)
When Jesus said, "I am he," they drew back and fell to the ground.

JOHN 18:4-6

The scattering rays of torchlight through the olive trees must have confused the sleepy disciples. They awakened with a jolt at the clamoring of at least two hundred men encircling them in the pale light of the full Passover moon.

As the armed men approach, a curious incident occurs. Jesus bravely goes out to meet them. The torches and lanterns indicate that they were expecting a search, certainly not expecting that the person they were looking for would be the first to confront them.

"I am," Jesus says. The Roman soldiers, as well as the Jewish priests and temple guards, fall to the ground. The Jews have heard someone speak the unspeakable Name. Perhaps the Roman legionnaires are simply awed at Jesus' command of the situation.

JOURNAL: *Write about that scene in the Garden of Gethsemane as though you were one of the disciples, then as though you were one of the priests or soldiers. How do the different perspectives add to your understanding of the scene?*

M O N D A Y

Sifted Like Wheat

"Simon, Simon, listen! Satan has demanded to sift all of you like wheat,
but I have prayed for you that your own faith may not fail;
and you, when once you have turned back, strengthen your brothers."

LUKE 22:31-32 NRSV

Like some New Testament parallel to the book of Job, Satan has come before the throne of God asking to inflict his worst on Simon. All the disciples will be sifted. But it is Simon Peter for whom Jesus specifically prays. All of them will go through the torture of seeing Jesus die on the cross. But Simon will be the one whose faith will ultimately not fail, all because of the prayers of his best friend, Jesus. He will repent, turn around and become a source of strength to his brothers. Peter, the fragile stone, strengthened by the prayers of Christ, will become a source of strength for his brothers and sisters of all the centuries ahead. It is Jesus' prayers that make Simon strong.

JOURNAL: *How do you respond to the idea that Christ intercedes for you?*

The Heartbreaking Denial

After a little while, those standing there went up to Peter and said,
"Surely you are one of them, for your accent gives you away."
Then he began to call down curses on himself and he swore to them,
"I don't know the man!"

MATTHEW 26:73-74

All four Gospels tell the story of Peter's denial of Christ. Each Gospel writer accounts for three denials—two initial queries followed an hour later by a third, more direct confrontation. The third query causes Peter not to curse but to swear an oath, something Jesus had urged them never to do.

Peter's denial would form an important message for the early church, faced with the same temptation to deny Jesus before their Roman persecutors. It is also the key to understanding the rest of Peter's life. Peter's heartbreaking denial provides an emotional window into the heart of the man he would become. It broke Peter in the best sense of the word.

JOURNAL: *When has fear made you pretend you are not a Christian or at least play down your identity with Christ?*

Peter replied, "Man, I don't know what you're talking about!"
Just as he was speaking, the rooster crowed.
The Lord turned and looked straight at Peter.

LUKE 22:60-61

Upon Peter's third denial, only Luke tells us that Jesus turned and looked at him across the courtyard. As their eyes met, Peter remembered Jesus' prediction that he would deny him. I believe it was this look that broke Peter's heart.

Luke uses a specific word for Jesus' glance. It is the same word John used to describe the first time Jesus looked at Peter. It means *to see with your mind, to understand.*

The understanding gaze of Jesus could not have been one of disdain or condemnation. That was not Jesus' way. After all, Jesus would be condemned for Peter. I believe the only look that could have broken Simon as it did was one of love and forgiveness. It is just what we would expect from the Savior.

JOURNAL: *How have you experienced the Lord's forgiveness and restoration after you have denied him?*

He Looks at Us

> *God demonstrates his own love for us in this:*
> *While we were still sinners, Christ died for us.*

ROMANS 5:8

Upon first seeing him, Jesus knew all there was to know about Simon, son of Jonah. And just now, seeing Peter at his absolute worst, Jesus is willing to turn and go to the cross for Peter—and for you and me. After all, he sees us just the same way he first saw Peter. He gazes at us with that understanding stare and sees all our potential, all our frailties and faults. And yet he was willing, even while we were still sinners, to take up that cross for us.

If, every time we read these passages about the failure and heartbreak of Peter, our hearts don't at the same time break a little more, we have failed to interact with the details of Scripture at the level of our imaginations.

PRAY: *Give thanks to Jesus that he knows all about you and still loves you and was willing to give his life for you. Let your heart be broken with the certainty of his understanding and his mercy.*

F R I D A Y

Three Reminders

> *Prepare your minds for action; discipline yourselves;*
> *set all your hope on the grace that Jesus Christ will bring you when he is revealed.*

1 PETER 1:13 NRSV

Years after the crucifixion and resurrection of Jesus, Peter echoed the lessons he learned the night Jesus was arrested. His first letter, which is a treatise on suffering, shows that he finally came to understand that God's call is not to evade or destroy the source of the suffering but, as Jesus did that night, to embrace it with all the courage God makes available through faith. In Acts we see Peter living out this lesson. And the sting of being found asleep three times at his post echoes three times in his letters.

APPLY: *Reread the Scripture passage above, along with 1 Peter 5:8-9 and 2 Peter 3:17—the other instances in which Peter reflects on falling asleep. In what areas of your life are you most liable to let down your guard and allow sin to take over?*

Past and Future Crowns

His eyes are like blazing fire, and on his head are many crowns.

REVELATION 19:12

Jesus' crown of thorns was meant to be a joke. The Roman soldiers, bored with their assignment on the fringes of the Empire, were looking for something to pass the time. When the crazy rabbi from Nazareth was left in their hands, they had the chance to vent the frustration that had been building up ever since they were assigned to this god-forsaken place.

In his great revelation, John saw Jesus with other crowns on his head. The meek thorn-crowned One, who first entered the Holy City riding a colt, will return riding a magnificent white horse, wearing not one but many crowns. He who suffered so many injustices will return with justice. His eyes, which before were full of tears and pain, will blaze like fire. And the same ears that bore the angry shouts of the crowd will hear angels and the multitude of the faithful saying, "Crown him with glory and honor and power!"

PRAY: *You are in the presence of the One who is called Faithful and True, whose head wears many crowns. What would you like to say to him? Perhaps your response will be silent awe. What is he saying to you?*

56

MONDAY *We Were There*

> *I have been crucified with Christ and I no longer live, but Christ lives in me.*
> *The life I live in the body, I live by faith in the Son of God,*
> *who loved me and gave himself for me.*

GALATIANS 2:20

When I was a boy I was drawn to a particular picture of the crucifixion of Jesus. It seemed more realistic than any others I had seen. The expression on Jesus' face spoke not of pain but of the agonizing anticipation of pain. The painting was shrouded in shadows, with the only beam of light focused directly on Jesus.

It always puzzled me that only one person was lifting the heavy cross into place, a peculiar non-Roman character wearing a beret cocked to one side. Later I learned the painting was by Rembrandt, and the solitary person struggling to raise the cross was in fact a self-portrait.

The painting itself is extremely powerful. Understanding it in the context of the painter's life lifts its meaning to another dimension. It is Rembrandt's contrite confession of his own complicity in the crucifixion of Christ. It is more than a painting. It is a parable.

JOURNAL: *Our sins put Jesus on the cross. Imagine yourself at the crucifixion, not as one of Jesus' disciples but as one of his crucifiers. Can you bring yourself to think in such a way? How do you gain in appreciation and gratitude for the cross?*

The Miracle of No Miracle

Those who passed by hurled insults at him, shaking their heads and saying,
"You who are going to destroy the temple and build it in three days, save yourself!
Come down from the cross, if you are the Son of God!"

MATTHEW 27:39-40

If ever a moment demanded a miracle, it was this moment. The crowds are clamoring and calling out for it. So are the two thieves crucified on either side of Jesus. Above all, it would seem that common sense demands it. *Now is the moment. Now is the time to show them your miraculous power!*

In the course of Jesus' misunderstood life, this is the moment he is most misunderstood. The crowd still clamors for miracles. But he did not come to give them miracles; he came to give them himself. And on the cross he is doing precisely that.

The cross reveals to us that Jesus' greatest miracle was his refusal at that moment to perform a miracle at all.

PRAY: *Thank and praise the Lord for refusing to miraculously come down from the cross.*

The Cross in the Heart

May I never boast except in the cross of our Lord Jesus Christ,
through which the world has been crucified to me, and I to the world.

GALATIANS 6:14

There it is on the communion table: the shiny brass crucifix. And there it is again on the lapel of a business suit. And again, hanging from the ear of a heavy metal singer. And in the corner of a business card, and on the steeple of a church, and on the bumper of a car, and in the hotel lobby next to the Star of David, to show lodgers where they might worship. I went to school with a boy who had a cross tattooed under his eye.

The first known representation of Jesus on the cross dates from around A.D. 200, more than 150 years after the crucifixion! It took that long for Christians to get around to portraying Jesus on the cross. My guess is that they shied away from representing the cross because it meant too much. Maybe they wanted the cross to become a vivid reality, which could only be kept alive in their hearts, instead of a symbol around their necks or below their eyes.

JOURNAL: *Notice today the places you see a cross. Where does it seem most appropriate and meaningful? Where is it taken casually? Do you think the cross should appear in more places or fewer, and why?*

Three Questions

Did not the Christ have to suffer these things and then enter his glory?

LUKE 24:26

The trappings of the crucifixion had always puzzled me. Why was it necessary that a close friend betray Jesus? Why the crown of thorns, that grim tribute to humor? Why the cross—wasn't there some other way for him to die? I had been playing with those three questions, trying to make them sound lyrical, in other words trying to make them sound pretty. But they aren't pretty questions.

I had finished three verses of a song incorporating the questions. I had planned to write one chorus which would answer all three. That proved to be as impossible as the questions themselves. So I did the only thing a committed seeker of the Truth could do: I gave up and put them away in a drawer!

JOURNAL: *What seemingly impossible questions have you asked God? When have you had to give up, at least temporarily, on the answers?*

Three Answers

Let us fix our eyes on Jesus, the author and perfecter of our faith,
who for the joy set before him endured the cross, scorning its shame,
and sat down at the right hand of the throne of God.

HEBREWS 12:2

Weeks after I gave up and put away my three song verses, I was awakened in the night with three separate choruses going through my mind, something that had never happened before and has never happened since. To my trilogy of vain, cynical questions the Lord gave three unexpected answers:

Why did it have to be a friend?

Because only a friend comes close enough to cause such pain.

Why the thorny crown?

Because in this life, the only kind of crown the world would give such a Lover is a crown of thorns.

Why did it have to be a cross?

Because the cross is the place for a thief. And Jesus had come to steal the world's heart away.

Now each time I listen to the song, I hear two separate voices: my own pessimistic voice asking the meaningless *why* questions, and another gentler Voice speaking the wonderful answers.

A P P L Y : *Listen today for God's unexpected answers to your most difficult questions.*

The Unexpected Miracle

On the first day of the week, just after sunrise,
they were on their way to the tomb and they asked each other,
"Who will roll the stone away from the entrance of the tomb?"

MARK 16:2-3

Among all of Jesus' followers, not a single one expected him to rise from the dead! Mark tells us that the faithful women made their way to the tomb with spices *to anoint a dead body.*

The two Marys, along with Salome, wonder who will move the stone for them. When they get to the tomb, they discover that strong invisible hands have already rolled the heavy stone back. As they enter the tomb, expecting the worst, they encounter instead a young man dressed in white. Before they have a chance to ask the obvious question, he says, "You are looking for Jesus the Nazarene, who was crucified. He has risen! He is not here."

PRAY: *Praise the Lord that he is risen from the dead! Offer your praise with words, songs, instrumental music, artwork or any other way which comes naturally to you.*

MONDAY *Believing and Wondering*

> *They still did not understand from Scripture*
> *that Jesus had to rise from the dead.*

JOHN 20:9

When Peter and John arrive at Jesus' tomb, John hesitates at the tomb door, like any good Jewish boy, not wanting to contract uncleanness. Peter heedlessly enters the tomb. Then come the tantalizing details of the interior of the tomb. The grave clothes were lying in folds while the *sudorion*, the sweat cloth which covered Jesus' face, was folded up separately by itself. The tomb was empty.

Luke says Peter went away wondering to himself what had happened. John records that the sight was enough to convince him. He saw and believed! But there was a mustard seed of faith in Simon's heart, and so the fact that he was wondering to himself what had happened should encourage us. At least he was wondering!

PRAY: *Do you ever wonder if Jesus' resurrection is too good to be true? Invite Jesus Christ to make his resurrection known to you and give you assurance that he lives.*

TUESDAY *An Unrecorded Meeting*

> *They got up and returned at once to Jerusalem.*
> *There they found the Eleven and those with them, assembled together and saying,*
> *"It is true! The Lord has risen and has appeared to Simon."*

LUKE 24:33-34

If the story should appear anywhere, it should be in Mark's Gospel. But it is nowhere to be seen there. Neither is it in Matthew or John. There is only the faintest hint of it in Luke. I refer to the first resurrection appearance to any of the disciples. It must have occurred some time after Peter's "wondering" episode outside the tomb.

It is impossible to know the content of that first meeting. Something deeply heart-wrenching must have taken place between Jesus and Peter. We can safely speculate that during that time together they somehow dealt with Peter's failure. Perhaps he fell at Jesus' feet and confessed that he was not the one to lead the disciples.

Whatever happened, we never again hear a word of Peter's denials. When he next sees Jesus, he will be so unhindered in his emotions that he throws himself into the lake and swims a hundred yards to shore. That was the act of a joyfully forgiven man.

If Jesus had not been raised, Peter would never have known such forgiveness. And neither would, neither could, we.

JOURNAL: *Jesus appeared to Simon Peter alone and restored him after his failure. Put yourself in Peter's place. What do you say to Jesus? What does he say to you?*

The New Dimension

> *On the evening of the first day of the week, when the disciples were together,*
> *with the doors locked for fear of the Jews,*
> *Jesus came and stood among them and said, "Peace be with you!"*

JOHN 20:19

It was that same old lesson again. In one sense it might have been Jesus' most important lesson, apart from teaching them who he was. They needed to hear it again and again, even as we require hearing it over and over.

The lesson: the call of Jesus is to look beyond what seems to be the reality of the situation to a new dimension of faith. The disciples have before them the embodiment of this new reality. In resurrected flesh and bone and blood, Jesus stands before them. He encourages them to touch him and understand the warm reality of his resurrection. He even eats a piece of fish for them, almost like a parlor trick, to show them that this—that he—is real. And because he is alive and real, everything he has promised them can be seen now to be true.

APPLY: *For the disciples, the apparent reality was that Jesus was dead; the truth was that he had risen! What apparent realities of your situation get you down? Take courage that Christ is alive and is with you.*

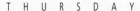

T H U R S D A Y

Known by His Scars

Let no one cause me trouble, for I bear on my body the marks of Jesus.

GALATIANS 6:17

When Jesus wanted to be recognized after his resurrection, he showed his disciples his scars. He didn't point to his face and say, "Look, it's me!" He showed them his hands and feet and side and gently said, "Look, it's me." Jesus is known by his scars. When we stand in his presence, he won't point to his face but to his scars and say, "Look, it's me."

Modern-day heretics point to material wealth and say, "Look, it's Jesus!" But the true followers of all ages will tell you, "This is Jesus, for I bear in my own body the marks of his death." As Jesus' resurrected body was recognized by its scars, so his body, the church, should be known by its scars and tears and the unspeakable joy it knows in spite of, and indeed because of, it all.

JOURNAL: *How do you respond to the popular idea that Christians are not supposed to suffer? What scars have you incurred as a result of following Christ?*

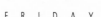

After a Hopeless Night

> *"I'm going out to fish," Simon Peter told them, and they said,*
> *"We'll go with you." So they went out and got into the boat,*
> *but that night they caught nothing.*

JOHN 21:3

How many times had he walked back into their lives after a hopeless night of fishing? And now, this one last time, he appeared again. Their nets were once again as empty as their hearts and souls. It was almost as if their last three years together had never really happened. Here they were, back where they started on the calm morning lake with empty nets after working all night.

Jesus appeared to them again where it all began three years earlier, on the shore of the lake. The ones who were to fish for people were fishing, unsuccessfully, once more for fish. All at once there he stood, not in glory with the legions of angels he said he commanded, but by a charcoal fire he himself had built with those ruined hands.

APPLY: *How are you tempted to go back to your previous ways before you met Christ? What if you suddenly realized he was "standing on the shore" watching you?*

Early in the morning, Jesus stood on the shore, but the disciples did not realize that it was Jesus.
He called out to them, "Friends, haven't you any fish?"
"No," they answered.
He said, "Throw your net on the right side of the boat and you will find some."
When they did, they were unable to haul the net in because of the large number of fish.

J O H N   2 1 : 4 - 6

As the disciples guide their boat to shore, their hearts as empty as their nets, they see a stranger standing on the sand. The stranger asks a pointed question, a question which in Greek expects the answer "No."

"Children, you haven't caught any fish, have you?"

"No," the disciples shout back.

"Throw your nets to starboard," he calls out.

"Why not," they mutter to themselves as they oblige the stranger.

And then it happens . . . again. Suddenly the boat lists hard to starboard and the ropes creak. Peter almost loses his footing. John bends over the side, both hands tight on the net. Looking not at Jesus but at the fish-filled net, he gasps, out of breath, "It's the Lord!"

J O U R N A L : *When has the Lord surprised you with his presence and his unde-served blessings?*

MONDAY *A Sudden Splash*

> *We did not follow cleverly invented stories*
> *when we told you about the power and coming of our Lord Jesus Christ,*
> *but we were eyewitnesses of his majesty.*

2 PETER 1:16

The disciple John, seeing the net full of fish, remembers that this happened once before. "It's the Lord!" he gasps. The next sound they hear is a splash, as impetuous Peter dives in and swims to shore.

There is something in me that is glad Peter responded that way. We might think he'd swim in the other direction since he had denied even knowing Jesus only a month or so earlier. But Peter, unlike Judas, seems to have known that forgiveness was waiting for him there on the shore.

JOURNAL: *When have you expected punishment and then realized you would be met with forgiveness? How did you respond?*

TUESDAY

A Hundred-Yard Swim

Then the disciple whom Jesus loved said to Peter, "It is the Lord!"
As soon as Simon Peter heard him say, "It is the Lord," he wrapped his
outer garment around him (for he had taken it off) and jumped into the water.

JOHN 21:7

John's short gasping phrase "It's the Lord!" is all Peter needs to hear. This time we do not hear Peter boldly asking if he might walk on the water. He gets to Jesus the best and fastest way he can. He throws his fisherman's coat on and dives into the chilly water. There was not a molecule of reluctance in his heart. He *had* to get to Jesus. What's a hundred-yard swim in the cold morning water if it means being beside *him*?

Peter sprints from the water's edge, splashing everything, including Jesus, like some sort of retriever. He stands a few feet in front of him, bent at the waist, hands on his knees, terribly out of breath. He hesitates for two seconds and then enfolds Jesus in his cold, soaking embrace. There are tears in both their eyes. If it had been a hundred miles instead of a hundred yards, Peter would have still gladly crossed them for this moment.

PRAY: *In your heart, rush to Jesus as Peter did, and receive Jesus' embrace of forgiveness.*

Breakfast on the Shore

Jesus said to them, "Come and have breakfast." None of the disciples dared ask him,
"Who are you?" They knew it was the Lord.

J O H N   2 1 : 1 2

By now the others have made it to the shore, towing the tremendous catch. Only now does Peter notice the smell of the bread and fish already cooking on the coals. A few weeks earlier he might have protested, "Lord, you shouldn't have done this," but now he knows better. Jesus smiles at the others and invites them to bring along some of the fish they have caught. Peter turns and performs the herculean task of dragging the net to shore, full of 153 large fish, all by himself!

They stand before Jesus in a loose semicircle, a strange expression on all their faces except Peter's. *Is it really him?* No, they know it's Jesus.

The meal is uncharacteristically quiet. Certainly no one argues this time about who is the greatest. That has been settled. The greatest, they now understand, has just prepared their breakfast like a common servant although he is the Lord of Glory.

A P P L Y : *How does the humility of Jesus speak to you? Where are you tempted to take pride even in your service?*

Do You Love Me?

When they had finished eating, Jesus said to Simon Peter,
"Simon son of John, do you truly love me more than these?"
"Yes, Lord," he said, "you know that I love you."
Jesus said, "Feed my lambs."

JOHN 21:15

The first call to become fishers of men and women had come there beside the sea. Now comes the call to be a shepherd. Peter might secretly think his love for Jesus is superior to all others. Perhaps it was. But love is seen only in obedience. Even as Jesus has fed them fish and bread, as indeed he has been feeding them for three years, so now Peter is to take the lead in feeding the lambs. And what is he supposed to feed them? Why Jesus, of course.

Jesus also says to Peter, "Take care of my sheep." Sheep, like people, need to be both fed and tended. That is the role of a shepherd. It will be the complete responsibility of Peter and all the apostles. *Shepherd* will become a major category for Peter in his letters. After all, that is what the word *pastor* means.

APPLY: *Who are the people you are called to take care of? How can you be a more conscientious shepherd for them?*

F R I D A Y

Leadership from Brokenness

Peter was hurt because Jesus asked him the third time, "Do you love me?"
He said, "Lord, you know all things; you know that I love you."

J O H N   2 1 : 1 7

He has commanded them to forgive. Now he will perfectly demonstrate forgiveness. His painful questions are meant to restore Peter to his proper place. They are an expression of Jesus' creative forgiveness. Jesus' questions open a wound in Peter's soul, a wound that can be tended to and healed only by being reopened. Now Peter understands that his position of leadership is founded not on his strength but on his brokenness.

It all took place beside a charcoal fire. The last time Peter had stood beside such a fire it was in despair and denial. Now it is a new world. And yet we can't help thinking that the smell of the coals in his nose was a powerful reminder of what had happened only a few days before. Now Peter knows forgiveness, restoration and the new privilege of a new call.

P R A Y : *Consider how Christ has forgiven and restored you. Thank him even for reminders of your previous failures, because they demonstrate the extent of his forgiveness.*

"Follow Me!"

Then he said to him, "Follow me!"

JOHN 21:19

There is no longer any misunderstanding on Simon's part. The remainder of his life will be spent living out Jesus' words. He will become the primary shepherd of the little, frightened flock of believers. He will care for them, risking his life to fend off the wolves. And he will feed them on Jesus' word.

They had first met beside this very same sea. At first Jesus had to show Simon that the lake he thought was empty was indeed full of fish. Now he has done it once again. Now a new kind of fisherman is left standing there, beside not a lake of fish but a vast sea of souls. He will fish for men and women. He will tend and feed the flock of Jesus. He can accomplish all this because, in his brokenness, he knows the certainty both of his love for Jesus and, more importantly, of Jesus' love for him. He is even armed with the painful knowing of his own death. He is ready.

PRAY: *Commit yourself to the role the Lord has for you, even if the specifics are not perfectly clear to you now.*

M O N D A Y *The Wind of the Spirit*

When the Day of Pentecost came, they were all together in one place.
Suddenly a sound like the blowing of a violent wind came from heaven
and filled the whole house where they were sitting.
They saw what seemed to be tongues of fire that separated and came to rest on each of them.
All of them were filled with the Holy Spirit
and began to speak in other tongues as the Spirit enabled them.

ACTS 2:1-4

The multilingual, multinational crowd has just heard in at least sixteen different languages what they can only describe as the "wonders of God." The specific content of what they heard in their own languages from the lips of the Galilean disciples is not recorded in the text. The point was not the content of the sermon the Holy Spirit was preaching through the disciples. The point was that God had now chosen to literally dwell in his people.

The Spirit had returned in power, like a violent wind. The presence of the Lord that had departed in the time of Ezekiel had at last returned (Ezekiel 10:18). It had not returned to fill a temple, however; the tongues of fire above each of the disciples' heads signified that they had all become living tabernacles.

JOURNAL: *Do you see yourself as a living tabernacle for the Holy Spirit? What difference does it make for you to know that God himself lives in you?*

What Shall We Do?

Therefore let all Israel be assured of this: God has made this Jesus,
whom you crucified, both Lord and Christ.

A C T S   2 : 3 6

Earlier, when God had spoken to encourage his Son, some of the people who heard the voice mistook it for thunder (John 12:29). Here the people are unable to grasp what the Lord is saying through this mysterious outpouring. Some of them try to write it off as drunkards under the influence.

In response to the confusion, Peter stands up and preaches his first sermon in Acts. He begins, as he will begin all his sermons in Acts, by announcing that the days of the fulfillment of God's purpose have arrived. He quotes an extensive passage from the prophet Joel, presumably from memory! Next he moves on to a brief account of the ministry of Jesus of Nazareth. Then follows a series of Old Testament quotes centering on David.

Peter must have summoned all the passion he could muster in the tone of his final statement: "God has made this Jesus, whom you crucified, both Lord and Christ!" Its impact on the crowd makes it clear. Luke tells us they were pierced (or stung) to the heart and cried out, "What shall we do?"

P R A Y : *Jesus is Lord and Christ. Ask him, "What shall I do?"*

WEDNESDAY

The Gift of the Spirit

*Peter replied, "Repent and be baptized, every one of you,
in the name of Jesus Christ for the forgiveness of your sins.
And you will receive the gift of the Holy Spirit."*

ACTS 2:38

The people's desperate response leads to the final section of Peter's first sermon. They must repent—turn completely around—and be baptized in the name of the very person they had a hand in nailing to the cross. Then, Peter tells them, they will receive the gift of the Holy Spirit, the very gift that has caused the entire ruckus in the first place.

This amazing promise is for them, for their children and for all who are far off, whom the Lord will call. At this early point in the ministry, there was no way Peter could see that the promise would spread as far as it eventually would, that he would be called on to extend it even across the vast distance of race to the Gentiles. The promise Jesus had spoken just before he had been taken up into heaven, that they would receive power and that they would become witnesses in Jerusalem, in all Judea and Samaria even to the ends of the earth, had begun to come literally true.

PRAY: *Do you feel weak or even powerless in certain areas where the Lord is calling you to obey? Allow him to empower you through the Holy Spirit.*

What I Have, I Give You

*Then Peter said, "Silver or gold I do not have, but what I have I give you.
In the name of Jesus Christ of Nazareth, walk."*

ACTS 3:6

Peter and John were still observing the three o'clock time of prayer at the temple. They were going there to pray and not to make sacrifices. For them the Sacrifice had finally and forever been offered! They are passing through the gate called Beautiful, the largest and main gate to the temple area. Beggars naturally congregated there.

When the lame man notices the two disciples, he calls out to them his well-rehearsed phrase. They turn and compassionately confront him. "Look at us!" Peter says. "Give us your attention. Do not regard us as simply sources of charity. We have infinitely more to give."

Peter and John are likewise penniless beggars, only they know Someone, and he is the wealth they have to give. Like Jesus, when Peter exercises the healing authority he has been given, he does not call attention to himself. There is no waving of arms, no magical incantation, only the pronouncement of a loving and authoritative word. Instantly the man's feet and ankles regain their strength and he leaps to his feet, jumping and praising God!

APPLY: *Who do you know that is begging for some bare minimum of attention? How will you offer the riches of Christ to that person?*

Turning the Praise to God

By faith in the name of Jesus, this man whom you see and know was made strong.
It is Jesus' name and the faith that comes through him
that has given this complete healing to him, as you can all see.

ACTS 3:16

Whenever Jesus healed the sick, people responded not by praising him but by giving praise to God. The humble, selfless way Jesus worked his miracles won praise not for himself but for his Father.

The same goes for Peter. We are told the man praises not Peter and John, but God. He recognizes that the power that has healed his lame ankles is not the possession of the simple man who has spoken Jesus' name; the power is in the name itself!

As at Pentecost, the miracle causes a commotion that needs to be explained. Peter immediately directs the attention away from themselves and toward the one whose power actually healed the man, Jesus. It was not their own power or godliness that made the healing happen.

PRAY: *Pray about any ways in which you want to take credit for what Christ alone has done. Ask for his forgiveness and for the humility to let all credit go to him.*

To Tell the Truth

Repent, then, and turn to God, so that your sins may be wiped out,
that times of refreshing may come from the Lord, and that he may send the Christ,
who has been appointed for you—even Jesus.

ACTS 3:19-20

In his sermons we hear the unadorned passion of Peter's heart. There is not a drop of pretense or self-awareness. He is not trying to posture or impress or even ultimately "win" his audience. What we hear is the heartfelt desire of a man who wants to tell us simply what he has heard and seen. He starts with the simplest truth about the good news: that it has come! He then tells us about Jesus, always appealing to the Scriptures that are life and breath to him. Finally, he calls out to his hearers and to us to turn around from the foolishness and sin we so recklessly follow to our own destruction, to realize that as much as any of the soldiers who stretched Jesus on the crossbeam and hammered the spikes into his hands and feet, we are responsible for his hanging there.

PRAY: *When you speak about your experience with Christ, what parts of the gospel do you tend to emphasize? What parts are you tempted to downplay, either through self-consciousness or through fear of your friends' reactions? Resolve to always speak truthfully from the heart when you share Christ.*

MONDAY

We Cannot Help Speaking

Then they called them in again and commanded them not to
speak or teach at all in the name of Jesus. But Peter and John replied,
"Judge for yourselves whether it is right in God's sight to obey you rather than God.
For we cannot help speaking about what we have seen and heard."

ACTS 4:18-20

Peter and John are dragged before the council and commanded to stop speaking in Jesus' name. Such a short time ago, in Caiaphas' own courtyard, Peter had denied knowing Jesus at all. Now in broadest daylight he courageously confesses that he cannot help himself. He must speak about all the things he has heard and seen. He will not refrain from speaking Jesus' name. How could he?

Luke told us about Jesus' prayer for Peter, that he would turn and strengthen his brothers (Luke 22:31-32). Here Luke presents the wonderful answer to that prayer. The two disciples are threatened once more but finally released. Peter will have another chance, a few days later, to finish the sermon that has been so rudely interrupted.

JOURNAL: *Write about places and circumstances in which you are reluctant to speak about Christ. Try to identify why you feel intimidated. Let your writings turn to prayer for courage to speak.*

TUESDAY

By What Power or Name?

The priests and the captain of the temple guard and the Sadducees came up to
Peter and John while they were speaking to the people. . . .
They had Peter and John brought before them and began to question them:
"By what power or what name did you do this?"

ACTS 4:1, 7

The court cannot condemn Peter and John for what they did. There was certainly no law against healing someone. So they take the direction of asking by
what authority or name the disciples had done what they had done. Their
hope is no doubt that the disciples will simply answer "Jesus of Nazareth"
(which they eventually will). But Peter, filled with the Holy Spirit, does not
provide a quick answer. He begins to preach to them.

Jesus had promised that they would be given the words to speak when they
were hauled in front of officials (Luke 21:13-15). This is the first example of
that promise coming true.

PRAY: *Thank the Holy Spirit for times that he has given you the right words in a*
time of crisis. Ask for confidence that he will continue to give you the right words at
the right time.

W E D N E S D A Y

The Gifts or the Giver?

More and more men and women believed in the Lord and were added to their number.
As a result, people brought the sick into the streets and laid them on beds and mats so that at
least Peter's shadow might fall on some of them as he passed by.

ACTS 5:14-15

As the number of Christians grew, so did the depth of their generosity and love. Luke tells us that they met together in a corner of the temple complex known as Solomon's Colonnade. Here they openly practiced the compassion of Jesus through healing everyone who was brought to them, as well as casting out demons.

The superstitious began to seek to have Peter's shadow pass over them. As happened during the ministry of Jesus, the people confused the gifts the disciples had to offer with the substance of what they most wanted to give. They were not, after all, simply healers. They had come to give the people Jesus.

APPLY: *What good gifts of the Lord have threatened to take precedence in your life over the Lord himself? How do you discern when this is happening?*

New Expectations

About that time [Tabitha] became sick and died, and her body was washed
and placed in an upstairs room. . . . Peter sent them all out of the room;
then he got down on his knees and prayed. Turning toward the dead woman, he said,
"Tabitha, get up." She opened her eyes, and seeing Peter she sat up.

ACTS 9:37, 40

Clearly Tabitha is dead before Peter is sent for. Her body has been washed and prepared for burial. Nonetheless, Peter is sent for with a totally new expectation. Though there is no word of his having done this kind of miracle before, the Christians beside the sea in Joppa fully expect that he can do it precisely because *Jesus did it.*

The new reality that Peter preached about came with an entirely new set of expectations. Already the truth of Jesus' life and resurrection had begun to take effect. Peter, who had stood by when Jesus raised Jairus's daughter from the dead, understood now and believed that because Jesus was alive and living in and through him in the person of the Holy Spirit, death had indeed lost its awful power. In Jesus it had become merely a sleep from which we will also someday awake when we hear those same words, "Get up."

APPLY: *What fears do you have about death, either your own or the death of loved ones? What difference does Jesus make in your outlook on death?*

Freedom in Jail

> *So Peter was kept in prison,*
> *but the church was earnestly praying to God for him.*

ACTS 12:5

Someone recently asked me to name my spiritual heroes. I mentioned Dietrich Bonhoeffer, Nicolae Moldovenu, John Perkins and a man I met in China whom I only know as Brother John. When I looked at the list I realized that the only thing they all had in common was that each one had been in prison for his faith. A modern-day philosopher has said, "The only way to deal with an unfree world is to become so absolutely free that your very existence is an act of rebellion." In so fallen and "unfree" a world as we live in, is it any surprise that those who possess the glorious freedom of Christ so often end up in jail?

In Luke 22:33 Peter had protested to Jesus that he was willing to go to prison for him. At least three times he would have the opportunity to make good on that promise.

JOURNAL: *Imagine that you are imprisoned for Christ. What would you pray for? What would be your greatest struggle? your greatest joy?*

An Angelic Thump

The night before Herod was to bring him to trial, Peter was sleeping between two soldiers,
bound with two chains, and sentries stood guard at the entrance.
Suddenly an angel of the Lord appeared and a light shone in the cell. He struck Peter on the side
and woke him up. "Quick, get up!" he said, and the chains fell off Peter's wrists.

ACTS 12:6-7

Three experiences of prison. First threatened, then beaten and perhaps—like James—headed for death. In each instance Peter is unmindful of the danger to himself. The very fact that, on the night before what he knows will be his execution, he can sleep so soundly that it requires a sound angelic thump on the side to waken him, reveals the profound courage Jesus had instilled in his heart and mind. And when Peter is released that morning, some ten years after the liberation of Jesus from the tomb, he moves out from Jerusalem and never looks back.

If the cold weight of the stone could not hold Jesus, then neither could the cruel iron bars of a prison cell. Peter experienced the freedom that all who have followed in his steps will testify to as well. The call is to live as free men and women no matter the circumstances, no matter how "unfree" a world we find ourselves living in.

PRAY: *Ask God for a free spirit no matter what your outward circumstances may be.*

Spring

MONDAY

The Urge to Create

> How many are your works, O LORD!
> In wisdom you made them all;
> the earth is full of your creatures.

PSALM 104:24

From the old lady who fills a page with doodling as she talks on the phone, to the man who welds together dinosaurs in the middle of the desert out of wrecked car parts, all around us are examples of this mysterious, powerful urge to create, to be creative, to live out or somehow respond to the beauty of our creative Father.

Perhaps you can look around your own home and see peculiar pots or pictures you've created because there seemed to be no other choice but to create them. People who cannot sing or play a note fill notebooks with songs. Others labor for decades over novels without the remotest hope of ever seeing them published.

We are driven to create at this deep wordless level of the soul because we are all fashioned in the image of a God who is an Artist.

JOURNAL: *How do you react to the idea that God is an Artist? What can you say about the art he has created?*

"Very Good!"

In the beginning God created the heavens and the earth.

GENESIS 1:1

When we first encounter God in the Bible, it is not as the awesome Lawgiver or the Judge of the universe but as the Artist. The language of Genesis is not flashy or grandiose; there is no waving of his great and powerful arm, no echoing of the mighty shout of the word of creation, no universe falling from his fingertips. Genesis tells us he stepped back from the canvas of creation at the end of each day to examine his work and, like any painter or sculptor, with the utmost simplicity declared, "Good."

Like an artist he begins with the more fundamental forms. The light and darkness, the earth, air and water are his pencil sketch. Next he moves up in complexity until at the top of the whole wonderful heap stands humanity. "Very good!" is his verdict.

JOURNAL: *How do you respond to the idea that humanity is God's "very good!" of creation?*

God's Masterpiece

> *God saw all that he had made, and it was very good.*
> *And there was evening, and there was morning—the sixth day.*

GENESIS 1:31

The image of God is woven into the fabric of everything we are. His thumbprint on our lives affects us in ways we will never begin to understand. His divine beauty, which is part of our essence as well, demands a response. We see a majestic sunset, and a line of poetry comes to mind, or an image to paint; or perhaps we merely give a sigh that can sound like a song.

Can a work like *Moby Dick* be understood in any other way? Is it not an extended, amplified sigh from the pen of Melville in response to the beauty and terror he experienced in the South Seas? Aren't the pages of such masterpieces merely signs that point us along in a direction toward the terrifying beauty of white whales and toward the God who created them?

When we ask this question, or any question akin to it, we will inevitably discover that God has already answered it in his Word, answered it before we ever thought to ask.

JOURNAL: *What aspects of the created world most readily turn you toward worship of the Creator?*

The First Lyric

> *The man said,*
> *"This is now bone of my bones*
> *and flesh of my flesh;*
> *she shall be called 'woman,'*
> *for she was taken out of man."*
>
> GENESIS 2:23

Even though he had been able to put a name to each of thousands of animals the Lord had paraded before him, Adam could not find a name for the ache he now felt in his bones. Later he would call it loneliness. But it must have been hard to understand the feeling of being lonely when what you are lonely for does not even exist yet. So before God created Eve, he must have created within Adam a lonely, empty place that was her exact shape and size.

When Eve is at last presented to Adam, her beauty demands a response, and so Adam sings the very first song: *This is flesh of my flesh, bone of my bones.* Adam's first lyric compliments and comforts Eve. It helps her to understand where she came from and where she is going, as well as who she is. And all art, ever since, has sought to do nothing more.

PRAY: *Thank God for the gift of song. Thank him for times you have been blessed through hearing songs and through singing.*

F R I D A Y
The First Creative Community

> *God blessed them and said to them,*
> *"Be fruitful and increase in number; fill the earth and subdue it.*
> *Rule over the fish of the sea and the birds of the air and over every*
> *living creature that moves on the ground."*

GENESIS 1:28

As the first couple, the first creative community, stands before their Creator King, they receive the creative mandate. It is more than a command to make a lot of babies, to become conservators of the earth. Neither is it a call to become "little gods," to somehow imitate God in the mystery of his limitless creativity. Rather, as romantic responders, Adam and Eve are encouraged not to answer back in some pale imitative way (real creativity is never imitative) but to give voice to their resonating hearts in praise. At its heart this is a call to worship.

JOURNAL: *What do you think it means that people are created in the image of God?*

Extending the Image

> *The LORD God took the man and put him in the Garden of Eden*
> *to work it and take care of it.*

GENESIS 2:15

The instruction to subdue and rule, as creature king and queen over God's creation, is a command to extend the image of God out into the world. Adam and Eve will create children who will carry on that image. They will plant gardens that will perpetuate the rich creativeness and beauty of God. They will continue creating and singing songs to one another, like Adam's first song to Eve. They will struggle to communicate their deep feelings to each other. When Cain, Abel and finally Seth come along, Adam and Eve will no doubt sing them to sleep. They will write poems to help them understand who they are and where they came from. And when the first gruesome murder occurs, the first dirge of suffering and sorrow will rise from their lips.

All these forms of creativity, even the weeding of the fields after the Fall, represent the varied creative ways that people can give themselves, offer themselves up. That is to say they are (or can be) forms of worship.

APPLY: *What are some avenues of creativity which you have not yet explored? What do you think holds you back?*

M O N D A Y *Preoccupied with Light*

This is the message we have heard from him and declare to you:
God is light; in him there is no darkness at all.

1 J O H N 1 : 5

Leonardo da Vinci's first memory was of being in his crib and having the tail of a kite come down and brush his face. He spent the rest of his life trying to learn to fly, both by means of various flying machines and parachutes, and—perhaps more significantly—by means of his amazing art.

My first memory is of taking a walk with one of my cousins. The grass was loaded with dew. When she pointed out the dew to me, I got down on my hands and knees and focused on a single drop through which the morning sun was shining. From that time on I have been preoccupied with light, or more exactly, with looking at and for light. It may be through the lens of a telescope, seeing the distant light of the stars, or reading in the pages of the Bible about Light that became a Person, someone who is at the same moment as distant as the stars and alive and shining inside me.

J O U R N A L : *What about God preoccupies your imagination? How does this sense of wonder affect how you pursue God?*

Astronomical Wonders

> *When I look at your heavens, the work of your fingers,*
> *the moon and the stars that you have established,*
> *what are human beings that you are mindful of them,*
> *mortals that you care for them?*

PSALM 8:3-4 NRSV

One night my son Will and I enjoyed a visual feast in the sky. We waited out the dusk, straining to see who would discover the first star. Then, all at once, there it was! Just as our eyes were beginning to get used to the sight, we looked over our shoulders and saw a dazzling full moon! It was as if, jealous for the attention, it had risen to steal our gaze from that first star. A few hours later the earth's shadow began to creep across the pockmarked face of that jealous moon in a full eclipse, turning it a deep brick red. For a finale, two meteors streaked across the sky, each leaving a sparkling trail.

Whenever Will sees these kinds of astronomical wonders he whispers to himself spontaneously, "Oh, thank you, Lord!" When I called him out later to see the eclipse, he looked up through sleepy eyes and whispered, "Praise the Lord for the moon!" Will is someone who has always been preoccupied with power and beauty. I believe it is a God-given preoccupation.

JOURNAL: *When have you taken special notice of the stars and the moon? What do they say to you about the character of God?*

The Beauty of the Lord

One thing I ask of the LORD,
this is what I seek:
that I may dwell in the house of the LORD
all the days of my life,
to gaze upon the beauty of the LORD
and to seek him in his temple.

PSALM 27:4

As we look at the stars, as we worship silently in the most massive cathedral of the summer sky, something in us aches and hungers and is not filled even in the presence of this awesome beauty. Our hunger for beauty is at the same time a hunger for love, for acceptance, which if you think about it long enough, you'll realize is a hunger for God. For he is beautiful.

Have you ever recognized your need for God in this particular way? We rarely ponder his beauty, much less seek to gaze upon it. Rarely does our theology include it in its outlines. But the beauty of God is a biblical reality. Throughout the Word of God he is recognized by and praised for being beautiful.

JOURNAL: *Write about the beauty of God. Are you accustomed to thinking of him as beautiful, or is this a new thought for you?*

The Reflection of Beauty

Clap your hands, all you nations;
shout to God with cries of joy.
How awesome is the LORD Most High,
the great King over all the earth!

PSALM 47:1-2

God's relentless movement toward us, his romantic reaching out in Christ, embodies a beauty beyond words. This divine beauty has been woven into the fabric of creation, in the massive stars, inside the submicroscopic balance of the atom. Though we grasp his beauty only in the most finite and rudimentary way, as creatures before a Creator, still it can be enough to incite an unconscious but uncontrollable desire to respond, to make our own personal world beautiful in its own way, to worship.

Creative worship is one appropriate response to the heartbreaking beauty of God. The beauty of his presence can be recognized and reflected in the beauty of our songs and dances. It can be seen in the fabric of our daily lives. A thousand examples speak of a deep, inner hunger for beauty that, at its heart, is a hunger for God. We hunger for beauty because it is a beautiful God whom we serve.

APPLY: *What is one way you can add beauty to your personal surroundings as a reflection of the beauty of God?*

FRIDAY *Beauty Has a Name*

The heavens declare the glory of God;
the skies proclaim the work of his hands.

PSALM 19:1

A young Chinese woman told me of the spiritual struggle of growing up in the shadow of communism, where official doctrine dictated against any belief in God. She said that ever since she was a little girl, her heart had resonated with the beauty of nature. First a sunset caused a deep stirring in her soul that she could not put into words. Then the beauty of the flowers in her mother's garden spoke to her of a simplicity for which her heart yearned. By observing the beauty in nature she became convinced of the existence of not simply a benign god but a loving, caring Father.

With tender, moist eyes and a brilliant smile she said, "Imagine the joy I experienced when I learned that he had a name and that it was Jesus."

JOURNAL: *When has the beauty of nature revealed Jesus to you and brought you closer to him?*

Creative Expression

> *Sing to the LORD a new song,*
> *his praise from the ends of the earth,*
> *you who go down to the sea, and all that is in it,*
> *you islands, and all who live in them.*

ISAIAH 42:10

The order, the balance and the beauty of creation are a shadow, like the shadow of the earth on the moon, which speaks of the essence of God. Such beauty draws us; it encourages and inspires us to worship. It even convicts us. The beauty of God demands a response from us.

Maybe your response is a poem or a symphony. Better yet, your response might take the form of a new and creative way to show someone your love and God's. That was Jesus' favorite form of creative expression!

PRAY: *Ask the Lord to show you how you can creatively express his beauty to someone else today.*

MONDAY

The Singing of the Stars

> *Where were you when I laid the earth's foundation . . .*
> *while the morning stars sang together*
> *and all the angels shouted for joy?*

JOB 38:4, 7

The singing of the stars is a song I have sought to hear for most of my life. Sometimes, by faith, I believe I hear it, singing of and to the Creator. It reminds me of the vastness of who he is. If the stars are singing, I am as certain as faith can be that they are singing a chorus to Christ, who made them and by whose immense, wordless power their mass is held together and kept burning so brilliantly. This chorus to Christ is a silent, wordless song, sung also with our lives and with whatever love we can lend to the chorus. It is an ancient, timeless, ever-new song.

JOURNAL: *If the stars sing a song with words, what might the words be?*

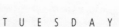

Early Songs

> *My heart is steadfast, O God;*
> *I will sing and make music with all my soul.*
> *Awake, harp and lyre!*
> *I will awaken the dawn.*

PSALM 108:1-2

It is the wee hours of the morning. Everyone is asleep but me. I have spent most of the day aimlessly moving words around on a piece of paper and taking inordinately long breaks to play computer games. Then, around two or three o'clock, when I run out of distractions, everything comes together. Often I realize that I have not taken time to ask for God's help or simply stopped to spend time with him.

All at once the words start to make more sense than anything I could have come up with on my own. They fit the melody like a glove, as if the song was somehow preexistent and I am only just now hearing it. I look at my watch and realize that what seemed only minutes took four or five hours, and the sun is rising. In the early dawn I play through a new song for the first time, singing it to myself and to God, as the stars sang the very first song to him.

JOURNAL: *When have you felt the Lord take over a project and make it come out far better than you could have imagined?*

A Song Never Sung Before

Praise the LORD.
Sing to the LORD a new song,
his praise in the assembly of the saints.

PSALM 149:1

As a songwriter I can tell you that the greatest moment of encouragement comes not from awards or high numbers on some chart but from the singing of a new song for the first time. To sing new words that have never been sung just this way before, to play combinations of notes that have never been heard, to wonder whether they will have the desired effect on the listener, whether people or God—the sharing of the new song is an experience unlike any other.

In the wisdom writings of the Old Testament (Psalms, Proverbs, Job, Ecclesiastes, Song of Solomon) we see excitement about the singing of a new song. The simple act of writing and singing something new demonstrates that the truth contained in the Scriptures can now be placed in the heart of the community as they sing together the truth of who God is. By singing the new song, they have made this truth their own.

APPLY: *The next time you sing with other Christians, imagine how the songs sounded to those who heard them for the first time. Notice how it affects your perception of the songs.*

In Response to a Hunger

Sing to the LORD a new song,
for he has done marvelous things;
his right hand and his holy arm
have worked salvation for him.

PSALM 98:1

In Scripture, whenever the kingdom is about to break through, there is always a rebirth of the new song. New songs are a major indicator that the Spirit of God is on the move, breathing, inspiring men and women to respond to his beauty for his sake as well as for the sake of the community of faith. New songs are a response to hunger, to God's desire to be praised for who he is and to the community's desire to be shown how to respond. By grace he gives us fresh material with which to worship him.

The psalmist understands this thirst. He sings of it again and again. He understands that the thirst is as much a part of God's blessing as the song that temporarily quenches the thirst.

PRAY: *Pray for a new song in your own heart, for a renewal of your first love for the Lord.*

FRIDAY

A Joyful Response

> *And they sang a new song before the throne*
> *and before the four living creatures and the elders.*

REVELATION 14:3

Without the need to create, without the preoccupation for newness, there would be no motivating force for the song. The need of the artist and the needs of the community are crucial to the creative process. God's desire for worship (it is impossible that God should need anything) is part of the fabric of the call to create new songs.

When God's Spirit moves, he leaves singing in his wake, and in particular he leaves new songs, songs that embody his truth and are an obedient response to his beauty. These songs are a spontaneous and joyful response to the great truth that it is in fact God who is doing something new! He is coming, and his approach is meant to be strewn, like palm branches, with new songs!

APPLY: *Today whenever you feel the desire to sing to the Lord, go ahead and sing, even if the time and place are unusual!*

Creativity as Worship

And whatever you do, whether in word or deed,
do it all in the name of the Lord Jesus,
giving thanks to God the Father through him.

COLOSSIANS 3:17

Creativity is worship because, at its essence, it is a response. I hear the Word and I respond with music, with silence, in adoration, in appreciation by picking up the basin and the towel. It is a romantic response to this Person whom I adore. He is beautiful! I want nothing more than to be in his presence. I love him! And so I sing and I write. If I could paint or dance I would do that as well. I forgive someone who couldn't care less about being forgiven. I try to reach out across the vast distance between me and my brother or sister.

Because creativity is a response, it does not originate with me. God speaks. He moves. He is beautiful. We respond. We create. We worship.

PRAY: *Ask the Lord to show you more creative ways to respond to him.*

MONDAY *An Artisan for God*

> *See, I have chosen Bezalel son of Uri, the son of Hur, of the tribe of Judah,*
> *and I have filled him with the Spirit of God, with skill, ability and knowledge*
> *in all kinds of crafts—to make artistic designs for work in gold, silver and bronze,*
> *to cut and set stones, to work in wood, and to engage in all kinds of craftsmanship.*

EXODUS 31:2-5

A remarkable feature of the tabernacle is the attention to detail: the precious metal for the post sockets, even the way knots were to be tied. Scholars have observed that the tabernacle contained every type of representational art: painting, woodworking, sculpting, weaving, metallurgy, ceramics and more.

The little-known individual named Bezalel is the first person in Scripture who is said to be filled with the Spirit. Bezalel becomes an artisan for God, equipped by the Spirit to create a place for God to dwell among his people. Bezalel thereby played a part in fulfilling the deepest desire in the heart of God.

Bezalel's experience is summed up in the two phrases God uses of him: "I have chosen" and "I have filled." His chosenness affirms the call of God on his life. His being filled indicates that God gave him the gifts required to fulfill that call.

PRAY: *Do you feel inadequate for your responsibilities? Pray that God's Spirit will equip you with all that you need, and trust him to do so at the right time.*

The Power of Imagination

*The LORD searches every heart
and understands every motive behind the thoughts.*

1 CHRONICLES 28:9

The sins that exercise the most control over us take place in the imagination. Jesus defined lust as taking place not primarily in dark alleys but in dark imaginations. Greed happens not when I make off with my neighbor's goods but when I imagine that they are mine.

The author of sin knows all too well the power of the imagination, so he too uses music, metaphor and vision for his grim purposes. He seeks to capture us as much as the Father seeks to recapture us.

Because we are called to creativity, a working, gut-level understanding of the imagination is vital. It can be our greatest strength or our greatest weakness. Sometimes it is both at the same time! To harness the imagination, or better yet, to bring it under submission to Christ, is something about which we don't talk or pray or do enough. But before it can be redemptively used, it must be reclaimed.

PRAY: *Confess sins which you commit in your imagination. Ask God to cleanse and take over your imagination.*

WEDNESDAY

Arguing with the Voice

> *Do not think of yourself more highly than you ought,*
> *but rather think of yourself with sober judgment.*

ROMANS 12:3

There is a voice that frustrates, befuddles and terrorizes me every time I sit down to write anything, whether a letter or a song. Sometimes it sounds like my own voice; at other times I do not recognize it at all:

"There is no conceivable way someone like you can create this."
"How can you possibly hope to do better than _____?"
"No one will listen or care what you have to say."
"Aren't you too tired?"
"What do you think you are, some kind of celebrity?"

I argue with this voice or I try to ignore it. I have found only one way to make it go away and leave me alone, and that is to shift my focus. Look again at the things it says. Each statement has one thing in common: "you."

Creativity is not about me or you. It is not us acting like little gods, creating on our own in the same way God creates. Creativity is a response to who God is.

JOURNAL: *What are the inner voices which intimidate you? What do they keep telling you? What difference does it make when you shift your focus from yourself to the Lord?*

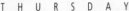

Choosing to Be a Celebrant

He must become greater; I must become less.

JOHN 3:30

One of the most irritating accusations my inner voice whispers is, "Do you think you're some kind of celebrity?"

By definition a celebrity is someone we celebrate. I looked it up. Just above the listing for *celebrity* I saw another word, *celebrant*. A celebrant is someone who officiates at the Eucharist. A celebrant is focused on Jesus and his sacrifice.

Today I choose to be a celebrant. By God's enabling grace I will hold Jesus up before the world and not hold myself up. I will seek to respond to his extravagant love by any and all means possible. I will strive to create art that will communicate to the world, and most especially to him, how much I love and long for his presence.

PRAY: *Pray that today you will be a celebrant who joyfully lifts up Jesus before the world.*

Constructive Criticism

The ear that heeds wholesome admonition
will lodge among the wise.
Those who ignore instruction despise themselves,
but those who heed admonition gain understanding.

PROVERBS 15:31-32 NRSV

When I began writing songs, I was a member of a small biracial church in Bowling Green, Kentucky. The pastor gave me outlines of his sermons and asked me to try to come up with songs or choruses. Whenever a song did come, I first shared it with him and received his responses, primarily about the lyrics. I also received immediate responses from my fellow church members when I performed the song.

The advice came from men and women whom I loved and deeply respected. Their words, even when they were critical, came in a context of support and trust. If they criticized a song, it was to help me write a better one next time. And so the songs—not only my own but those of the other writers in the church—gradually improved over time. The criticism was truly constructive.

JOURNAL: *How do you respond to criticism? How are you at giving constructive criticism? How can you improve on both counts?*

Creative Communities

Let the word of Christ dwell in you richly as you teach and admonish
one another with all wisdom, and as you sing psalms,
hymns and spiritual songs with gratitude in your hearts to God.

COLOSSIANS 3:16

The Bible gives us several examples of creative communities. In the Old Testament the music and craftsmanship of both tabernacle and temple worship came out of the community of artist-priests. As the phenomenon of prophecy grew, schools or families of prophets came together. Old Testament prophecy was almost certainly accompanied by music, so these prophetic schools were involved with prophetic music as well as words.

In the New Testament, as music passed from the professional priest-musician to the amateur lay-musician, the church became the center for corporate worship. Art and music were created in response to the needs of the community. The body of Christ became the repository for a vast wealth of creativity.

Community called creativity forth. Art, music, mercy and every form of ministry seen in the body are responses to the needs of the community. The need for kindness, beauty and truth cry out for each of us to wash the feet of the brothers and sisters with our various creative gifts.

JOURNAL: *How has the creativity of other Christians helped you worship God or understand Scripture? How can you allow God to use your creativity more fully?*

MONDAY

The Burden of the Prophet

But if I say, "I will not mention him
or speak any more in his name,"
his word is in my heart like a fire,
a fire shut up in my bones.

JEREMIAH 20:9

People often ask me, "What is the experience of song writing like for you?" In all these years I have not been able to come up with an adequate answer. Sometimes I tell them it is like prayer, because it primarily involves listening to God and to his Word.

The only experience the writing of every song has in common is what I call *a sense of being burdened.* Often there is a specific message with which I am burdened. More often, there is little or nothing specific. What I am to say is not clear to me. There is just the burden to say something. And God help me if I do not attempt to say it.

One of the Hebrew words for prophecy literally means "burden." Jeremiah speaks of this burden as a burning in the bones. Through the prophets we see God attempting to do what he will perfectly do through his Son and what he still longs to do in and through us: recapture our imaginations and set us on fire.

PRAY: *Pray that God will give you the urgency to speak his words and the courage to do so.*

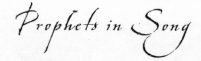

Prophets in Song

The word of the LORD came to me:
"Son of man, set forth an allegory and tell the house of Israel a parable."

EZEKIEL 17:1-2

The prophets use rich language and marvelous metaphors, the language of the imagination. Isaiah speaks of the sun and moon being ashamed; the trees clap their hands. We also see God speaking through the bizarre activities of the prophets. Jeremiah hides his linen belt and breaks a clay jar. Ezekiel constructs a toy town in the dust. Hosea knowingly marries a prostitute.

On a superficial level, we learn from the prophets that the tools best suited for communicating to the imagination are images, parables and sometimes even bizarre activity! At a deeper level, we learn that if we are to effect a permanent change in people's hearts, we must do more than teach them facts or reduce them to some emotional experience. We must reach out to the heart as well as the mind by speaking to the imagination.

JOURNAL: *What are your favorite parables or images in Scripture? Why do they speak to you so deeply?*

The Door of Our Imagination

Write down the revelation
and make it plain on tablets
so that a herald may run with it.

HABAKKUK 2 : 2

God is the Creator-Artist, the great Romancer, the perfectly loving Father. He calls out to us, sings to us, paints images in our minds through the prophets' visions. These sounds and songs stand at the door of our imagination and knock. Through them God opens the door of his own inner life to us. He paints pictures of his hopes for our future as well as his worst nightmares of what waits for us if we choose to go on living without him.

By the prophets' example we discover that God speaks through the parable of our daily lives, in the silence of prayer, in the good news of creation. They open our eyes to a vision as grand as the greatest of their own visions, to a world alive with God's speaking at every turn, in every moment, no matter how mundane. Through the prophets we begin to glimpse a God who loves us so much that he calls himself our Husband, who longs to embrace us as Father, who ultimately comes to us as Son.

PRAY: *Pray that you will be sensitive to what the Lord says to you today through what you see and hear, whether in nature, in things made by people, or in people's words and actions.*

No Exhaustive Explanation

*[Jesus] said, "The knowledge of the secrets of the kingdom of God has been given to you,
but to others I speak in parables."*

L U K E   8 : 1 0

The Greek word *parabolē* literally means "to throw beside." A parable happens when Jesus *throws* out a simple story and lets it fall *beside* a particular person in a particular situation.

The parables of Christ are a mystery. They are not equations to be solved once and for all. Even as no doctor can completely describe the way the blood flowing through our veins accomplishes the mystery of life, so there is no exhaustive explanation of parables. You are never "done" with a single parable of Jesus. Perhaps it is better to say, his parables are never done with you. The simplest parable will continue speaking for the rest of your life, if you choose to listen.

APPLY: *Choose one of Jesus' parables. Make a special effort to live by its truth today. Notice new depths of meaning you find as you put it into practice.*

The "Aha!" Moment

With many similar parables Jesus spoke the word to them, as much as they could understand.
He did not say anything to them without using a parable.
But when he was alone with his own disciples, he explained everything.

MARK 4:33-34

Most of the parables of Jesus exhibit a lack of closure. Yes, they have endings. The boy returns home, the judge finally listens to the widow, the pearl is found. But the moral of the story, the summation, the conclusion, is often left unstated.

Within the freedom of the form of the parable, Jesus leaves the "aha!" to us. The moment of realization is ours to savor, and if we explain the parables to death we rob them of this, their most important characteristic. The transcendent "aha!" moment of the opening of the eye of the heart is to be experienced by you alone with the Spirit.

JOURNAL: *Write about a time when you suddenly realized what God was trying to say to you. How did he get through to you? What did that "aha!" moment feel like? What happened as a result?*

Why Parables?

The disciples came to him and asked,
"Why do you speak to the people in parables?"

MATTHEW 13:10

The frustrated disciples asked, "Why don't you just say it straight out, Jesus?" It is a frustration most of us share, not only as we seek to understand the Bible, but also as we strain to hear God's voice in the parable of our daily lives. There is so little straight-out language in the Bible or in life. But it is so for a purpose.

Parables work because truth has been woven into the fabric of creation. Everyone understands the word pictures of a seed falling into the ground, of a parent loving a child, of a person anxiously searching for something valuable that has been lost. From such basic creation facts, eternal lessons can be drawn by means of parables.

PRAY: *Thank God that he makes you think. Thank him that his truth is all around you, and pray that you will be able to discern it.*

MONDAY

The Hiddenness of Humility

*God opposes the proud
but gives grace to the humble.*

JAMES 4:6

Artists in medieval times did not sign their work. Their art was a gift meant to point away from themselves and toward the God who gave it. They were safely hidden in Christ, free from the tyranny of the self. They knew the great truth that they were nothing more and nothing less than children of a great King who had been entrusted with a sacred task: to win praise for their Lord.

Knowing who we are is the hiddenness of humility. It is believing that the giftedness we may possess is not of our own making, that the purpose of its being given is not that we might gain attention or praise for ourselves, but that we might respond in gratitude with our best creative effort to win praise for the One who first gave the gift.

APPLY: *Consider the ways in which you are compelled to "sign your work," to make sure you receive credit for what you have done. How can you move into the hiddenness of humility and let God get the credit?*

What Are They Thinking?

What do you have that you did not receive?
And if you did receive it, why do you boast about it as though you did not?

1 CORINTHIANS 4:7

Let's say I have a concert coming up. I go to the hall full of myself, thinking only of what people will think of me. I have everything to lose, since all that I am is riding on my success. As I begin to perform, the songs flow at first, but then my mind starts to wander. *What are they thinking about me?* Just then I learn the painful equation: thinking of yourself equals messing up.

Now let's say I go into my concert with a pretty good feel for my ability. I may not be the best musician in the world, but neither am I the worst. Whatever gifts I have were given to me and are really not mine. As I play, my energy is not wasted on thinking of myself. The point is to present the message of the song, to "wash the feet" of people or even God by faithfully playing my best. Now I become the beneficiary of another equation: to forget yourself equals the best possible performance.

JOURNAL: *When have you experienced the equation that "thinking of yourself equals messing up"? When have you experienced the equation that "to forget yourself equals the best possible performance"?*

True and False Humility

The crucible is for silver, and the furnace is for gold,
so a person is tested by being praised.

PROVERBS 27:21 NRSV

"That was a good concert," someone will say to me.

"Oh no," I moan, "I sang flat, my guitar was out of tune . . ."

What passes for my humility is in fact only a disguised form of pride, a ploy to hear more compliments. At these moments I have forgotten who I am, and I look to strangers to tell me. I have lost sight of the truth of what Jesus has done in and for me. This is a perilous place to be, a dangerous trap.

Genuine, biblical humility is nothing more or less than knowing the truth of who we are in Christ. Only relationship with him can give us the genuine article.

APPLY: *Pay special attention to how you respond to compliments. Do you display false humility (pride in disguise) or genuine humility (security in your identity in Christ)?*

Free to Be Slaves of Christ

I tell you the truth, everyone who sins is a slave to sin.
Now a slave has no permanent place in the family, but a son belongs to it forever.
So if the Son sets you free, you will be free indeed.

JOHN 8:34-36

Jesus said that knowing the truth about who we are sets us free. But being set free in an upside-down kingdom means being set free to become a servant. Before we were granted this freedom we were slaves to ourselves, that is, slaves to sin. Now, having been set free from ourselves, we are free to be slaves for Christ.

This newfound freedom is an experience of unveiling, of seeing not only oneself but also one's giftedness for the first time. "What do you have that you did not receive?" Paul asks. In the light of this new freedom of humility, knowing the truth of who we are, we answer that our giftedness is not our own, it is from our creative Creator God. You and I stand unveiled as the recipients of a gift that is beyond ourselves.

PRAY: *How do you respond to the idea of being a "slave" to Christ? Ask him what tasks he has for you today. Do those tasks as to him and not to any ordinary human master.*

Hopeless yet Full of Hope

Who will bring any charge against those whom God has chosen?
It is God who justifies. Who is he that condemns?
Christ Jesus, who died—more than that, who was raised to life—
is at the right hand of God and is also interceding for us.

ROMANS 8:33-34

Jesus reveals two crucial truths about ourselves. In the tension between these truths lies real humility. On the one hand he convicts us of our sin and fallenness, telling us our righteousness is really only filthy rags. And then in the next breath, smothering us with a big hug like the father of the prodigal son, he tells us how much we are valued, that in spite of our rebellion he loves us so much that he would rather die than live without us.

That is who I am. And that is who you are as well if you know him. We are men and women, boys and girls who are truly hopeless yet full of hope, truly lost but nonetheless truly found. We are shored up on either side so there is no room for false humility on one side or pride on the other.

PRAY: *Agree with the Lord that you are fallen and that he still loves and accepts you. Tell him how you feel about his amazing love.*

The Humility of Jesus

I tell you the truth, the Son can do nothing by himself;
he can do only what he sees his Father doing,
because whatever the Father does the Son also does.

JOHN 5:19

The humility of Jesus is evident on every page of the Gospels. Though he might have grasped equality with God, Jesus lets go of position and authority. He comes in poverty and weakness. He always points away from himself and directly to the Father upon whom he says again and again he is totally dependent. As a result, when Jesus performs a miracle he is never praised for it. He always wins praise for the Father.

The humility of Jesus is most strikingly portrayed in his miracles. Without question they are literally miracles. They shatter and defy nature, physics and the world as we know it. But if you listen closely to the text, you will notice that Jesus' manner, his demeanor, the way in which he does his miracles is ordinary and simple. There is something decidedly unmiraculous about his miracles.

JOURNAL: *Consider the miracles of Jesus. How do they display his humility and his dependence on the Father?*

MONDAY

Did You Miss It?

*By myself I can do nothing; I judge only as I hear, and my judgment is just,
for I seek not to please myself but him who sent me.*

JOHN 5:30

Jesus' first miracle, turning water into wine, was recognized by only a few slaves at the wedding feast in Cana. "Go fill up those water jars," he said. Then, "Now take it to the master of ceremonies." Did you miss it? The miracle happened. We could say the same about the feeding of the five thousand. There was no shouting, no waving of arms in the air, no hocus-pocus. Jesus simply prayed and passed the food out.

Jesus performed his miracles in a way that always miraculously directed the attention away from himself and toward the Father. Jesus healed someone who was sick, and those who witnessed the healing inevitably praised God. Jesus won praise for the Father, not himself. Indeed, Jesus was not ashamed to confess his total dependence on God.

APPLY: *If Jesus was not ashamed to confess his total dependence on God, how do your words and actions compare with his? How will you express your dependence today?*

Jesus said to the servants, "Fill the jars with water"; so they filled them to the brim.
Then he told them, "Now draw some out and take it to the master of the banquet."
They did so, and the master of the banquet tasted the water that had been turned into wine.
He did not realize where it had come from,
though the servants who had drawn the water knew.

JOHN 2:7-9

John tells us that through changing water into wine, Jesus revealed his glory (John 2:11). But when we look closely at the character of the miracle, there is little that is glorious about it. This is not to say that the miracle was not miraculous. But I'd like to emphasize the character of Jesus' performance of the miracle, indeed the way he performs almost every miracle.

"Fill the jars and take them over there," he simply says.

"What miracle?" the bystanders might have asked.

"The master of the banquet tasted *the water that had been turned into wine.*"

No magic formula (because the Lord of the Universe doesn't need magic!), no self-glorification; and yet John says this is how Jesus reveals his glory.

This is Jesus' way. This is how he wins praise for God.

JOURNAL: *Put yourself in the place of the master of the banquet. What do you think when you realize what has happened? How do you react? What (if anything) do you say to Jesus?*

Transformation of the Ordinary

This, the first of his miraculous signs, Jesus performed at Cana in Galilee.
He thus revealed his glory, and his disciples put their faith in him.

JOHN 2:11

When we examine the miracles, a consistent image of Jesus of Nazareth comes into view. It makes sense that the One who refused to grasp equality with God would perform most of his miracles in such an unmiraculous, almost hidden way. It fits the paradox of his life. Power through weakness, wisdom through foolishness, total victory through bloody defeat.

In our case Jesus often begins a miraculous change with a simple command, "Follow me," or "Don't be afraid." The wedding at Cana teaches us that he is ready to transform every ordinary element in our lives into the glorious stuff of miracles. But this first miracle prepares us for the fact that the world around us will usually fail to appreciate or even see it at all.

An unrecognized, unappreciated miracle is no less miraculous for not being seen. Jesus Christ has begun a hidden transformation in you, from death to life. Isn't the inner change in your life more glorious than the transformation of water to wine?

JOURNAL: *How has Christ transformed your life? What further transformation would you like him to make? How will you cooperate with him to bring that about?*

You Give Them Something

By this time it was late in the day, so his disciples came to him.
"This is a remote place," they said, "and it's already very late. Send the people away so they can
go to the surrounding countryside and villages and buy themselves something to eat."
But he answered, "You give them something to eat."

MARK 6:35-37

The disciples have returned from their first mission. They excitedly report back to Jesus, but they're exhausted, and he is marvelously aware of it. They seek refuge in a remote place, only to find that as many as 15,000 hungry men, women and children have followed them into the wilderness.

The ludicrous command of Jesus, "*You* give them something to eat," is meant to prepare us for the miracle to come. The miracle of the loaves and fish seems so unmiraculous that many scholars argue that there was no miracle at all. They suggest that the generosity of the one who provided the loaves and fish simply inspired everyone else to share their food as well. When we look at the story, it's not hard to understand why they could reach such an erroneous conclusion. After all, what does Jesus do? He simply says the blessing.

PRAY: *Bring to the Lord any needs for which you do not have the resources—whether spiritual, physical, emotional or financial. Ask him to provide. Keep your eyes open for an inconspicuous miracle.*

"How many loaves do you have?" he asked.
When they found out, they said, "Five—and two fish."
Then Jesus directed them to have all the people sit down in groups on the green grass.
So they sat down in groups of hundreds and fifties.
Taking the five loaves and the two fish and looking up to heaven,
he gave thanks and broke the loaves. Then he gave them to his disciples to set
before the people. He also divided the two fish among them all.

MARK 6:38-41

Jesus asks, "What do you have?" The small amount of food the disciples can scrape together is absurdly inadequate in the face of the multitude. Yet Jesus is always ready to use our absurd inadequacies. That is what makes it a miracle!

The rabbinic blessing or *barocha* for the meal was *"Blessed art thou, eternal God our Father, who causes bread to come forth from the ground."* After the *barocha* comes the straightforward command to pass out the food. Mark does not record the response of the crowd, whether they recognized a miracle had occurred or not. Could it not be that, even as at Cana, only the servants (in this case, the disciples) knew a miracle had occurred?

APPLY: *Where do you feel absurdly inadequate? Ask Jesus to give his blessing, and go ahead with what you need to do.*

Just Enough

> *They all ate and were satisfied, and the disciples picked up*
> *twelve basketfuls of broken pieces of bread and fish.*

MARK 6 : 42 - 43

After the feeding of the multitude, Jesus tells the disciples to pick up the leftovers, known in Judaism as the *peah*. Mark tells us that they gathered twelve small lunchpail-sized baskets of crumbs. The leftovers were just enough to provide for the twelve disciples. Does the fact that they could gather only twelve small baskets of crumbs from such an enormous crowd seem striking to you, even miraculous in an unmiraculous sort of way?

Sometimes the miracle is "just enough" provision. Jesus taught us to pray, "Give us this day our daily bread." Can we not praise him just as much for giving us exactly what we need, as we can when he provides an abundance?

JOURNAL: *When has God given you exactly what you needed, and it was "just enough"? Did you recognize his provision at the time?*

MONDAY

"Hallelujah!"

> *Hallelujah!*
> *Salvation and glory and power belong to our God,*
> *for true and just are his judgments.*

REVELATION 19:1-2

In Scripture, rejoicing is always tied to either what God has done or what he has promised he will do, an event that often includes the destruction of the wicked. He has revealed in his Word that vengeance is his, and his alone. It is his decision to exact vengeance on the one "who corrupted the earth by her adulteries" (Revelation 19:2). And the multitude in heaven begins to rejoice and shout, "Hallelujah!" No one in the heavenly crowd seems squeamish about fully celebrating what God has done.

In the New Testament the word *hallelujah,* which literally means "praise be to Yahweh," is found only in Revelation, where it is the keynote of the great multitude in heaven in chapter 19. They shout "Hallelujah!" not merely over the downfall of the evil one but because of who God is, because of his salvation, power and glory. They shout "Hallelujah!" because at last his reign is established forever and the wedding of the Lamb has come!

APPLY: *How many ways can you say "Hallelujah!" to God today?*

Parties Break Out

> *The Son of Man came eating and drinking, and they say,*
> *"Here is a glutton and a drunkard, a friend of tax collectors and 'sinners.'"*

MATTHEW 11:19

At funerals I have often heard preachers say that it is really a celebration. They usually aren't very convincing, least of all to those closest to the deceased.

My grandmother's funeral was a celebration. It was an outright party! What was supposed to be a wake quickly turned into a party that grew so loud that two employees of the funeral home had to finally come in and ask us to quiet down out of respect to the other clients. Had it gone on, the police would have no doubt been called in to arrest us for disturbing the peace.

Wherever and whenever Christians come together, parties should break out because we follow a Savior who is preoccupied with them. Whenever Jesus wasn't preaching or teaching you'd find him at a party. It might be at a tax collector's or at a Pharisee's home. The guests might include powerful men in the community or the riffraff. What seemed to bother the stuffy "religious" types wasn't that Jesus went to parties, but that he seemed to enjoy himself too much!

APPLY: *When you and your fellow Christians get together, is there a festive atmosphere? How can you infuse more joy into your worship and fellowship?*

The Party Goes On!

They broke bread in their homes and ate together with glad and sincere hearts,
praising God and enjoying the favor of all the people.
And the Lord added to their number daily those who were being saved.

ACTS 2:46-47

Jesus' first miracle was at a wedding at Cana in Galilee, where he turned water into wine, some four hundred gallons of it! I have heard many explanations of this miracle, but I think they miss the point. The point is that running out of wine was the surest way of bringing the party to a grinding halt, and Jesus' provision allowed the party to go on.

The concept of the party was important not only to Jesus but to the early church as well. The fellowship of the early Christians was a primary source of evangelism. They enjoyed the favor of all the people as the pagans witnessed the joy of their gatherings.

The climax of the history of this world will take place at a party. It is the Marriage Supper of the Lamb, and it will quite literally be the party of all time. There Jesus, the Bridegroom, will at last be brought together with us, his Bride, at a party where no one would dream of coming in and telling us to quiet down.

JOURNAL: *If the Marriage Supper of the Lamb will be the party of all time, what do you think it will look like? Sound like? What scents will waft among the celebrants? What expressions do you think will be on people's faces? What will be the center of attraction of the party?*

Revealed to Children

At that time Jesus, full of joy through the Holy Spirit, said,
"I praise you, Father, Lord of heaven and earth, because you have hidden
these things from the wise and learned, and revealed them to little children.
Yes, Father, for this was your good pleasure."

LUKE 10:21

The seventy-two, a select group of disciples which only Luke mentions, have just returned from a successful mission. They exclaim to Jesus that even demons submit to them because of the power of his name. It is perhaps the most joyful, exuberant moment in Jesus' ministry.

Now Jesus reveals the source of his joy: the Father has hidden such things from the wise and revealed them to little children. God is the One who is behind the radical reversal. Those who should "get it" (the wise) don't, because God has chosen to hide it from them. At the same time the simple, childlike people have been the beneficiaries of God's gracious revelation. And something about this facet of his Father's character causes the joy to overflow in the Son's heart.

PRAY: *Thank the Lord for the children in your life. Pray that you will be more like them in the simplicity of your trust.*

Occasions of Joy

> *And while they still did not believe it because of joy and amazement,*
> *he asked them, "Do you have anything here to eat?"*

LUKE 24:41

Joy is hard to find on ordinary days, in the routine of daily life. If real joy is to be found, it must come from the outside. On those mystical occasions when joy comes to us from beyond, the ordinary is transformed into a vehicle for true joy. The entire world can be transformed in a moment. A trip to the grocery store can quickly change into an adventure. Changing a dirty diaper can become a meaningful demonstration of divine love. A sterile hotel room far from home can be transformed in an instant into a holy place where you might even be confronted with the risen Lord.

The first Easter began as an ordinary day. Jesus chose an ordinary day to transform the world and give us the chance to know joy.

JOURNAL: *When have you suddenly encountered joy in the middle of routine? What did the experience tell you about God?*

Saved from Drudgery

If you obey my commands, you will remain in my love,
just as I have obeyed my Father's commands and remain in his love.
I have told you this so that my joy may be in you and that your joy may be complete.
My command is this: Love each other as I have loved you.

JOHN 15:10-12

Jesus saves us not only from our sin and ourselves. He also saves us from our ordinariness. He transforms the drudgery of daily existence into a wonderful journey with him. We see with new eyes, hear with new ears.

An ordinary voice can become sweet. A simple flower is seen to possess the mystery of life. We find meaning where there was no meaning before, precisely because Jesus brings new meaning to everything, even the most meaningless of days. We find joy where before there was only dullness of heart because, beyond ourselves, Jesus has come, the true bringer of joy.

PRAY: *Pray that your dullest tasks will be transformed with the joy of Christ. Invite him to show himself to you in the midst of drudgery. Pray that your eyes and ears will be open to him.*

M O N D A Y

"Teach Us to Pray"

One day Jesus was praying in a certain place.
When he finished, one of his disciples said to him,
"Lord, teach us to pray, just as John taught his disciples."

LUKE 11:1

For a time I was absorbed in reading books about prayer. But in the end I discovered that the best way to learn about prayer is to pray. And the best way to pray is to become a good listener and allow the Other to speak.

We all have friends who dominate the conversation. Are you that sort of friend to God? After all, who has the more worthwhile things to say?

Sometimes it is helpful to break old habits. If your prayers seem long, simply pray the Lord's Prayer. The simplicity of it will be refreshing, and more time will be left for listening. Remember, Jesus gave this prayer in response to the same petition that is on your heart: "Lord, teach us to pray."

P R A Y : *Today, try praying in some different way or with different words or in a different place or posture.*

Confidence and Certainty

> [Jesus] said to them, "When you pray, say:
>
> "'Father,
>
> hallowed be your name,
>
> your kingdom come.
>
> Give us each day our daily bread.
>
> Forgive us our sins,
>
> for we also forgive everyone who sins against us.
>
> And lead us not into temptation.'"

LUKE 11:2-4

After all the emphasis on prayer in the Gospel of Luke, we are anxious, like the disciples, to simply hear Jesus pray. So they ask, "Lord, teach us to pray." And we are glad that they asked. Jesus offers a prayer (the shorter form of what we call the Lord's Prayer), stunningly brief and simple yet bottomless in its implications. It can be spoken in a single breath. A child as well as a Ph.D. can learn to pray by means of this prayer.

Jesus' emphasis is not so much on what we say, on "getting it right." He focuses instead on the confidence and certainty we can have in God, who as our Father, knows what we need.

APPLY: *When you pray, are you ever preoccupied with getting the right words? Pray spontaneously without worrying about how you express yourself. Try praying out loud, or try writing or drawing or singing your prayers.*

Wandering Minds

Be still, and know that I am God;
I will be exalted among the nations,
I will be exalted in the earth.

PSALM 46:10

While I was at Western Kentucky University, Eberhard Bethge, the great biographer of Dietrich Bonhoeffer, shared a story with us. Bonhoeffer was discipling a group of young men in a secret underground seminary during World War II. The regimen required students to meditate on a passage of Scripture for two hours a day.

After only a few days, some of the men complained to Bonhoeffer that their minds were wandering. It was unreasonable, they told the amused Bonhoeffer, to require this of them when they had so many worries at home. He told them to stop trying to fight it. "Follow your mind wherever it goes," he said. "Follow it until it stops and then, wherever it stops, make that person or problem a matter for prayer. The struggling only leads to more noise and inner turmoil."

APPLY: *As you read Scripture, take Bonhoeffer's advice and follow your wandering mind wherever it goes. Make that person or problem a matter for prayer. Then return to the Scripture.*

Listening in Prayer

One of those days Jesus went out to a mountainside to pray,
and spent the night praying to God.

LUKE 6:12

Though Jesus' divinity possessed the very mind of God, his humanity continually sought out the Father in all-night prayer sessions. In the account of those sessions we hear very few words, so we can assume that there was much listening. But not listening for answers, for information. Prayer, for Jesus, seems to have been a time for simply sharing the presence of his Father, listening to the silence of his breathing. When his cousin John is murdered, he flees to the arms of prayer. When he is confronted with the conflict of wills between his Father and himself, it is precisely his Father he flees to in the garden.

Jesus' life of prayer teaches us that we do not merely listen for words; we must learn to listen to the silence.

P R A Y : *Does silence in prayer upset you? Bring your concerns to the Lord and then simply wait in silence.*

F R I D A Y *The Gift of His Spirit*

If you then, though you are evil, know how to give good gifts to your children,
how much more will your Father in heaven give the Holy Spirit to those who ask him!

LUKE 11:13

God knows how to give good gifts. He is the One who finds the seekers, who answers the askers, who opens the door of his life to those who knock.

What is God's great gift, according to Jesus? What is the present he chooses to give to his children? It is the Holy Spirit!

Jesus teaches us that what we ask for in prayer is rarely what we need. We usually ask for provision, when the God who knows how to give good gifts is ready to give us his presence through the Holy Spirit. And so the prayer he gave us, that can be spoken in a single breath, is rooted in the request for his breath, for his Spirit.

JOURNAL: *What do you think of when you see the words "Holy Spirit"? What does the Holy Spirit mean to you? How have you experienced the Spirit?*

"Son of David, Have Mercy!"

As Jesus approached Jericho, a blind man was sitting by the roadside begging.
When he heard the crowd going by, he asked what was happening.
They told him, "Jesus of Nazareth is passing by."
He called out, "Jesus, Son of David, have mercy on me!"

LUKE 18:35-37

Years ago I wrote lyrics to a song about the Lord's Prayer. The title was "The Perfect Prayer." It is perfect simply because Jesus himself spoke it. But there is at least one other perfect prayer in the Gospels and we find it here. Like Jesus' prayer, it is painfully short. It contains only seven words. "Son of David, have mercy on me!"

We must see this story from a first-century perspective. Everyone would have believed that the man was blind because he had done something to deserve it. Obviously he had sinned, and sinners do not deserve anything. When we understand this, we begin to see that the disciples in the front of the crowd were perfectly justified in trying to shut the man up.

APPLY: *Whom do you consider most deserving of God's attention? Whom do you consider least deserving? Reflect on the fact that Jesus stopped for those whom the crowds considered least deserving.*

M O N D A Y   *Stubborn Insistence*

> *Those who led the way rebuked him and told him to be quiet,*
> *but he shouted all the more, "Jesus, Son of David, have mercy on me!"*

LUKE 18:39

Jesus should not have had time for such people. The blind man's stubborn insistence to keep on crying out to Jesus is what makes me love him so much. I believe it's why Jesus seems to have been delighted by him as well. He sits there forsaken, in his own dark world, crying out for a gift he knows he does not deserve. He cries out for mercy. His cry is the perfect prayer, because it is the simplest request for what is most critical. It asks from God what is most essential. It is a plaintive cry for a piece of God's own heart.

PRAY: *Bring your most urgent needs to Jesus and pray, "Son of David, have mercy on me!"*

The One from Whom We Ask

Now on his way to Jerusalem, Jesus traveled along the border between Samaria and Galilee.
As he was going into a village, ten men who had leprosy met him.
They stood at a distance and called out in a loud voice, "Jesus, Master, have pity on us!"

LUKE 17:11-13

The story of the blind man who cried out for mercy comes at the end of Luke's Gospel. Jesus is on his way to Jerusalem. He knows that the cross is waiting for him there. Only one chapter before, Luke told us the story of the ten lepers. Their cry was almost the same as the blind man's: "Jesus, Master, have pity on us!"

Jesus told the ten to go and show themselves to the priests. While they were on the way, they discovered they were healed. Only one of them, a Samaritan, turned and ran back to Jesus, "praising God in a loud voice" (Luke 17:15). In his humility, Jesus told the lone leper exactly what he told the blind man: "Your faith has made you well." It was the faith to ask for something you know you do not deserve, believing in the nature of the One from whom you are asking.

PRAY: *Have you received blessings from God and neglected to thank him? Take time to thank him now.*

An Unimaginable Alternative

Praise be to the God and Father of our Lord Jesus Christ!
In his great mercy he has given us new birth into a living hope
through the resurrection of Jesus Christ from the dead.

1 PETER 1:3

Jesus is about to enter Jerusalem and undergo the Passion. There on the cross he will perfectly demonstrate what mercy is all about. He will show the world what the mercy of God looks like. He will demonstrate that God longs to lavish his mercy on us so much that he will sacrifice his only Son.

Through Jesus, God will offer the world an unimaginable alternative. To those of us who have a right to expect nothing, Jesus will offer everything. The doorway to an infinite store of mercy can be opened by seven simple words, "Son of David, have mercy on me."

APPLY: *How will you show God's mercy to someone else today?*

This Table Is for You

> *When the kindness and love of God our Savior appeared, he saved us,*
> *not because of righteous things we had done, but because of his mercy.*

TITUS 3:4-5

I remember the exact spot where I sat that particular Sunday morning in college. Our pastor, Bill Lane, began talking about sin. The theological wheels in my head began to turn, responding, interacting, even challenging his various points.

Then Dr. Lane began to list particular sins. "There are young couples in the congregation this morning who are not married but who have nonetheless spent the night together." Dr. Lane's list went on and on. With his wonderful skill with language he made the subtler sins sound just as sinful as the more blatant ones, which of course they were. When he finally came to the end, he repeated the list in condensed form.

After Dr. Lane's second volley, he seemed about to go through the list yet a third time. "If you are guilty of such and such," he said as we all braced ourselves, "If you are guilty . . ." he paused, "If you are guilty, then this table is for you." He pointed to the communion table in front of the pulpit. The service setting seemed to be bathed in light, its simplicity almost painful to look at.

JOURNAL: *What sins would Dr. Lane have mentioned that would have pierced your heart? What would you have thought as he directed your attention to the communion table?*

The Welcome of Jesus

Examine yourselves, and only then eat of the bread and drink of the cup.

1 CORINTHIANS 11:28 NRSV

When Dr. Lane pointed to the communion table and said, "This table is for you," I wanted to rush forward and seize the elements, like someone who had been lost in the wilderness, ravenously hungry and desperately thirsty. For the first time in my life, communion became *Holy Communion*. It meant life and peace and joy. The rough hands of the elderly black deacons now placed before me a treasure worth selling everything for. It was all mine, for free!

The call to examine our sins before we take communion is not there so we can make a full accounting of our sins and thereby be worthy to come to the table. That call to judge ourselves helps us realize that we have no right whatsoever to be there! You and I, we are the prostitutes and the tax collectors Jesus welcomed to fellowship with him. The lunatic joy I felt comes only from seeing that we have no right to come to the table at all, but Jesus welcomes us as his special guests, to be astounded at his generosity.

APPLY: *Think about your attitude when you take communion. Are you aware that you have no right to be there, yet Jesus still welcomes you? Resolve to keep both truths in mind the next time you take communion—and every time.*

I Am Invited

> *While Jesus was having dinner at Matthew's house, many tax collectors and*
> *"sinners" came and ate with him and his disciples. When the Pharisees saw this,*
> *they asked his disciples, "Why does your teacher eat with tax collectors and 'sinners'?"*

MATTHEW 9:10-11

Often, when I celebrate the Lord's Supper, I remember the question of the Pharisees at Matthew's house: "Why do you eat with tax collectors and sinners?" At those moments I hope I'm recovering just a bit of the experience of Matthew and his friends. For Jesus has invited me, a sinner, to share the table with him. It makes me deeply glad that Jesus is the unorthodox One who came looking, not for the righteous ones, but for someone like me.

At communion I find myself at the table with the Lord himself. There are sinners at every place, most especially mine. Still I find times when I join the Pharisees and look down on others, thinking myself better than they are. At such moments, the Lord reminds me with his Word of just who he is—and who I am.

APPLY: *Have you ever looked down on someone else taking communion? Search your heart for the reasons why. Ask the Lord to forgive you and to remind you that all who take communion are undeserving.*

MONDAY

The Foolishness of the Gospel

God was pleased through the foolishness of what was preached to save those who believe.

1 CORINTHIANS 1:21

Looking at the gospel straight on, it is foolish. An itinerant Galilean carpenter says he is God. A virgin birth. A resurrection after three days. Apart from the Spirit's enabling us to have faith in the wisdom of it, these things are impossible to believe.

I tend to be suspicious of people who try to make these impossible concepts make sense. Some of the greatest minds in the history of the world have embraced the gospel, but they were always ready to confess the inadequacy of the human mind to grasp the wisdom of God and therefore the absolute necessity for faith. That is not anti-intellectualism, but humility.

All the wisdom of God is found in Jesus. That is foolishness to human beings. Even as Paul played the fool with the so-called super apostles, so we are called to follow the One who played the fool for our sake.

PRAY: *Admit to God that there are things about the gospel that you don't understand. Submit to his wisdom.*

A Wisdom to Worship

We preach Christ crucified: a stumbling block to Jews and foolishness to Gentiles,
but to those whom God has called, both Jews and Greeks,
Christ the power of God and the wisdom of God.

1 CORINTHIANS 1:23-24

I used to see wisdom as something to possess, as a commodity, a thing. I suppose that's why I went to college to study philosophy. I am thankful that early in those college years I began to discover that there was more to wisdom than the accumulation of facts and information. Although I hadn't found out what true wisdom was, at least I was given the grace to recognize its impostor.

Wisdom is not the ability to be correct all the time. Genuine wisdom is concerned with a life well-lived. Wisdom isn't something we know as much as something we become.

Christians have found a wisdom not to ponder but to worship, a wisdom that is not a matter of words but who is the Word. This wisdom has everything to do with life because he is the Life. He gives us wisdom because he gives us himself.

JOURNAL: *What do you think it means to be wise?*

Does It Make Sense?

There was a man who had two sons. The younger one said to his father,
"Father, give me my share of the estate." So he divided his property between them.

LUKE 15:11

We know the prodigal son story so well that we think we understand it, that we have gotten to the bottom of it. But the parables of Jesus are bottomless. If you do not arrive at some new dimension each time you read them, you're not really listening.

Try looking at the old father from a different point of view, as a fool, for that is what the parable's first hearers would have thought. He was a fool to divide his fortune and give the share to the younger brother before his death. In fact, by dividing his estate he was giving away a big part of his own retirement. He was a fool to linger in the road, looking for the prodigal to come back. He was a fool to come running, believing the lame little speech the boy had practiced all the way home. And to add to what he has already thrown away on the boy, the old man pulls out all the stops and throws a party.

Does this make any sense at all, to shower such generosity on such a person?

JOURNAL: *Consider the father in Jesus' parable in Luke 15. Which of his actions are foolish by the world's standards?*

A Shocking Mercy

But while he was still a long way off,
his father saw him and was filled with compassion for him;
he ran to his son, threw his arms around him and kissed him.

LUKE 15:20

If you are able to make this shift in your imagination and see the old man as a fool, be prepared for a shock. The foolish old man in Jesus' story is clearly God. This is a parable of *hesed*, an untranslatable Hebrew word sometimes rendered *mercy, lovingkindness, covenant-faithfulness* or *love*.

I experience *hesed* when the one from whom I have a right to expect nothing, gives me everything. The wayward boy had no right to expect anything except a door slammed in his face. The best he could hope for was a stern lecture, a beating and maybe a second chance.

But there stands the ridiculous father in the middle of the road. There's no telling how long he has been there, straining towards the horizon. When he sees the familiar silhouette, limping home, he sprints towards him. There is a robe over his arm and a ring in his pocket. The boy who has a right to expect nothing is about to receive everything. He is hopeless and hungry. He is you and me. And the foolish, doting old man is our heavenly Father.

PRAY: *Thank God for being your patient, yearning, welcoming, merciful Father.*

FRIDAY *A Hater of Mercy*

The older brother became angry and refused to go in.
So his father went out and pleaded with him.

LUKE 15:28

Almost every time Jesus presents a lesson on mercy, he includes someone in the story I call a "hater of *hesed.*" Whenever someone is pictured repentant and receiving grace, Jesus paints someone else in the shadows who simply hates the fact that God acts in such ways. Mercy means the salvation of some and, inexplicably, the damnation of others. The older brother in the parable is a hater of *hesed.*

The first hearers of Jesus' parable would have sooner sided with the older brother than with the prodigal. After all, he stayed home, obedient and hard-working. He didn't demand anything at all, not his inheritance, not even his father's love. No, he would earn that.

JOURNAL: *Why do you think God's mercy provokes some people to anger?*

But he answered his father,
"Look! All these years I've been slaving for you and never disobeyed your orders."

LUKE 15:29

When the prodigal finally came home, imagine the older brother's disappointment. The father did not respond in justice, but in the mercy the older son was beginning to hate. Didn't the older brother have every right to be disappointed? But then so did his father. It seems apparent that his father gave up his rights along with his retirement funds. The father does not seem to know how to hold on to things, only how to let them go.

The prodigal returns begging only to be made a slave. The father will hear nothing of it. Then the older brother exposes himself. "I have been *slaving* for you," he whines. It is the kind of radical reversal Jesus loves to employ. The hopeless son who deserved slavery is mercifully restored to full sonship, while Jesus reveals that the older son has really been a slave all along. He has been enslaved by his hatred for the loving kindness of his generous and noble father.

APPLY: *Have you ever felt like the older brother in the parable, feeling that you have earned God's blessings, and resentful of God's mercy toward someone else? Ask God to transform your heart so you see yourself as undeserving yet welcomed back.*

154

M O N D A Y *A Lavish Repentance*

> *When a woman who had lived a sinful life in that town learned that*
> *Jesus was eating at the Pharisee's house, she brought an alabaster jar of perfume,*
> *and as she stood behind him at his feet weeping, she began to wet his feet with her tears.*

LUKE 7:36-38

Though Simon had invited Jesus to his home, he had neglected the common courtesy of providing water and a towel so Jesus could wash his tired feet. Perhaps because he was still not sure just whose side Jesus was on, he also neglected to greet him with the customary kiss. Finally, he had failed to provide Jesus with refreshing oil with which to anoint his head.

At some point during the meal, a sinful woman makes her way to the place directly behind the reclining Jesus. As she stands behind Jesus, caught up in the power of conviction, she begins to weep, her tears falling on his unwashed feet. Seeing what she had done, she kneels and in an extraordinary gesture of intimacy, takes down her hair and wipes her tears away. After she had wiped her tears away, she poured an expensive bottle of perfume on Jesus' now-clean feet.

Simon the Pharisee, who knew his Bible better than you and I could ever hope to know it, completely misses the point. Meanwhile the last person we might have expected, the sinful woman, fully understands her sin and her need for Jesus.

JOURNAL: *Put yourself in the place of the Pharisee. What do you think of the woman's actions? What do you do and say?*

When the Pharisee who had invited him saw this, he said to himself,
"If this man were a prophet, he would know who is touching him
and what kind of woman she is—that she is a sinner."
Jesus answered him, "Simon, I have something to tell you."

LUKE 7:39-40

Jesus does not condemn Simon. Listen to the tenderness in his voice. "Simon, I have something to say to you . . ." Jesus overlooks the fact that Simon has judged him. He tells the Pharisee a simple parable about two debtors, both of whom had their debts canceled. Simon agreed that the one with the bigger debt would love the lender more.

Then Jesus asks the Pharisee, "Do you see this woman?" (v. 44). By means of Jesus' parable, Simon begins to truly see. Too often we judge others by our "seeing" when we need focus only on the feet of Jesus.

APPLY: *What kind of people do you most quickly judge, and why? How can you see them as Jesus sees them?*

One Creditor, Two Debtors

"A certain creditor had two debtors; one owed five hundred denarii, and the other fifty.
When they could not pay, he canceled the debts for both of them.
Now which of them will love him more?"

LUKE 7:41-42

Jesus' brilliant parable is only two verses long, yet it can stand alone as a work of literary art. But when we see it in context, the story provides a place for all of them; the woman is the great debtor, Simon, the one who owed less. We are also meant to take our place in the parable, which is also an invitation to find our place at Simon's banquet. Will we sit beside Jesus and acknowledge only a small debt? Or will we fall down at his feet and in tears beg for the forgiveness we do not deserve?

The gentleness of Jesus' story led the Pharisee, like a lost sheep, to a place of understanding he could never have reached otherwise. We cannot say for certain if Simon, like so many other Pharisees, eventually became a disciple of Jesus. What we can say for certain is that his blind eyes started to see, which is no less a miracle.

APPLY: *What is your place in Jesus' brief parable?*

Spiritual Vision

> *Then he turned toward the woman and said to Simon, "Do you see this woman?"*

LUKE 7:44

All Simon can see are his theological categories: a prophet (Jesus) and a sinner (the woman). Like many of the religious people of his day and ours, Simon is functionally spiritually blind.

But what about the woman? What does she see? She sees her own sin and is clearly repentant. She sees Jesus and knows he is the only person in whom she will find forgiveness and restoration. She sees his feet and an opportunity to worship him. She wets his feet with her tears, wipes them with her hair in an amazing demonstration of intimacy and pours thousands of dollars worth of perfume on them. For the clarity of her spiritual vision, Jesus forgives her sins.

Jesus turns to Simon and pointedly asks, "Do you *see* this woman . . . ?" For the truth is, he had not. Jesus, who loves stubborn Simon as much as the woman, longs for him to really see her, not as a category, not as a "sinner," but simply as a needy person who needed to be loved and forgiven.

PRAY: *Pray for the Lord to remove any spiritual blindness concerning yourself, others or him. Pray that you will always come to Jesus in repentance rather than hang back in stubbornness.*

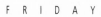

Desperate Boldness

> *As soon as she heard about him, a woman whose little daughter*
> *was possessed by an evil spirit came and fell at his feet.*
> *The woman was a Greek, born in Syrian Phoenicia.*
> *She begged Jesus to drive the demon out of her daughter.*

MARK 7:25-26

Once again Jesus has fled the draining presence of the crowd to get some rest. Once again he discovers that, even for him, this is an impossibility. A desperate woman barges into the silence that surrounds the exhausted Jesus. She frantically falls at his feet, begging for a miracle.

Like the Roman centurion who asked Jesus to heal his servant, this woman recognizes Jesus' authority. But note that it does not create a fence between them. Though she might have perceived him, a Jewish rabbi, as unapproachable, even in his tiredness Jesus is open to her. Rabbis were not even supposed to speak to women in public, much less Gentile women. But Jesus engages the worried woman in an unforgettable conversation.

PRAY: *Is there some problem about which you have been reluctant to pray? Bring it boldly to the Lord now.*

A Crumb from the Table

"First let the children eat all they want," he told her,
"for it is not right to take the children's bread and toss it to their dogs."
"Yes, Lord," she replied, "but even the dogs under the table eat the children's crumbs."
Then he told her, "For such a reply, you may go; the demon has left your daughter."

MARK 7:27-30

To us Jesus' reply sounds harsh. In Judaism dogs were looked upon as unclean animals. But Jesus does not use the word for *stray dogs*. He uses the diminutive term for *little dogs* or *pet dogs*. In the Greek woman's world it was common to keep small pet dogs. The image of children throwing scraps of bread to their pets underneath the table does not offend her in the least. In fact, it has the opposite effect. Her charming but stubborn response delights Jesus. It represents an imaginative expression of her faith in him.

When she returns home, she senses that the dark demonic cloud is gone. Her little girl is lying quietly in bed, no more convulsions, no more self-destructive behavior. Her home and her family will never be the same, and all this represents just a crumb that has fallen from the table!

JOURNAL: *Imagine that you are the Greek woman rushing back home. You walk into your house and discover that your daughter is well again, free of the demon. What do you think? Do? Say?*

MONDAY

Open Our Earlids

> *[An expert in the law] wanted to justify himself,*
> *so he asked Jesus, "And who is my neighbor?"*

LUKE 10:29

By itself, the story of the Good Samaritan would be a spiritual classic. Given the context in the Gospel of Luke, it is nothing less than transformational. Though Jesus had recently been kicked out of a Samaritan village he had intended to visit (Luke 9:52-53), he bore them no ill will. In his parable, one of their own would be the representative of the loving kindness of God.

Jesus' parable teaches us that we never really know anything until we understand it at the level of the imagination. The legal expert has all the right answers in his head but nothing in his heart. The parable will once more provide the means for the miracle of the opening of blind eyes. Jesus' story opens his "earlids" so that his eyelids can begin to open as well.

JOURNAL: *When have you discovered that you had right answers in your head but not in your heart? What brought you to that realization?*

Scandalous Reversal

> *"But a Samaritan, as he traveled, came where the man was;*
> *and when he saw him, he took pity on him. He went to him and bandaged his wounds,*
> *pouring on oil and wine. Then he put the man on his own donkey,*
> *took him to an inn and took care of him."*

LUKE 10:33-34

Hatred between Jews and Samaritans had been smoldering ever since the Jews returned from the Babylonian exile. It erupted time and time again until finally in 128 B.C. the Jews burned the Samaritans' rival temple to the ground.

In the parable of the Good Samaritan, Jesus provides two opportunities for the religious contingent to do the right thing. But both the priest and the Levite cross to the other side of the road to avoid the anonymous victim. Then comes the shocker. The Samaritan stops and shows compassion, binding the robbery victim's wounds and pouring oil and wine on them. Once they reach the inn, he provides two days' wages to cover any costs involved in taking care of the stranger, and he pledges to return and cover the rest.

In a scandalous reversal, those who should, don't; and those who shouldn't, do.

APPLY: *Have you ever acted as the priest or the Levite and passed up an opportunity to do the right thing? Is there a way you can remedy the situation now?*

A Neighbor or Not?

"Which of the three do you think was a neighbor to the man who fell into the hands of robbers?"
The expert in the law replied, "The one who had mercy on him."
Jesus told him, "Go and do likewise."

LUKE 10:36-37

When Jesus asks which of the three had done the right thing, the legal expert cannot even bring himself to say the word *Samaritan*. All he can mutter is the circumlocution, "the one who had mercy." Once again the religious professionals, the ones who should have "gotten it," fail miserably, while the last imaginable person, a Samaritan, responds the way God himself would respond.

The roads I travel every day are lined with those who are dying and yet I cross to the other side, I roll up my windows and turn on the radio. I pray that I will truly see who is my neighbor. By God's grace, I don't want to be in the category of those who should "get it" but don't.

PRAY: *Pray that the next time you have an opportunity to be a neighbor, you will "get it" and take advantage of it. Ask God to show you a specific opportunity today.*

Doing the Impossible

Love your enemies, do good, and lend, expecting nothing in return.
Your reward will be great, and you will be children of the Most High;
for he is kind to the ungrateful and the wicked.
Be merciful, just as your Father is merciful.

LUKE 6:35-36 NRSV

We've read the words so many times that their paradox and unorthodoxy have drained right out of them. What we need to recover from the Scriptures is just how impossible a command Jesus is making. Most of us can't even do a decent job of loving our friends and family, much less our enemies. But central to Jesus' unorthodoxy are his demands to do the impossible: to love our enemies, to be merciful even as God himself is merciful.

JOURNAL: *How do you respond to Jesus' command "Love your enemies"? What have been your experiences with trying to obey this command?*

An Unfinished Sermon

Be wise in the way you act toward outsiders;
make the most of every opportunity.

COLOSSIANS 4:5

My friend and pastor Denny Denson was in the middle of a sermon one Sunday morning when a young man he had been witnessing to for months slipped into the back of the church. The young man was a victim of crack cocaine and had more than once tried to get off the drug, promising to someday attend our church. When Denny saw him walk in that morning, he was hopeful and excited that he had come.

After a few minutes the young man got up and walked back outside. Denny understood at once what he needed to do. He stopped in the middle of his sermon and asked the congregation to go to prayer. With that, he followed the man outside and caught up with him a block from the church. After perhaps fifteen minutes the two of them came back inside with good news. The young man had finally accepted Jesus as his Lord and Savior. The remainder of the service was spent in worship. Denny never finished his sermon!

APPLY: *Are you willing to be interrupted for the sake of someone who needs the Lord?*

Giving Through Brokenness

Come to me, all you who are weary and burdened, and I will give you rest.
Take my yoke upon you and learn from me, for I am gentle and humble in heart,
and you will find rest for your souls. For my yoke is easy and my burden is light.

MATTHEW 11:28-30

If Jesus is truly our paradigm and pattern, then like him we must constantly search for new and creative ways to give ourselves to others for his sake. That is true creativity. It does not require perfect pitch. It does not demand digital dexterity. It does not demand anything at all except surrender.

This is not to say that it is easy. There is a level of giving that we achieve only through brokenness, but the burden is light precisely because the One who places it on our lives never completely takes his hand from under the weight. He never stops pursuing us, even to the last moment of our lives. He creates a space in time that allows us to hear, understand and respond to his extravagant invitation.

PRAY: *Offer yourself to the Lord. Ask him to be your strength as you give yourself to others for his sake.*

Summer

M O N D A Y *Servant and Apostle*

Simon Peter, a servant and apostle of Jesus Christ.

2 PETER 1:1

Peter is fully himself, whatever Gospel you take up. His rich and complex character stays the same whatever Gospel you read. He is the most human of the apostles. Perhaps that's one reason Jesus seemed to be so attracted to him. Indeed, it is the same reason we are still attracted to him today. It's a miracle, when you think about it, that Jesus would be able to choose a person whom so many of us could relate to, feel a kinship with and love.

A great way to come closer to someone is to get to know the person's best friend. The depth of the friendship between Jesus and Peter is beyond question. And it is Jesus I desire most deeply to know. Peter would not have it any other way.

JOURNAL: *What do you think it would have been like to be Jesus' best friend?*

A Witness to Christ

To the elders among you, I appeal as a fellow elder,
a witness of Christ's sufferings and one who will also share in the glory to be revealed.

1 PETER 5:1

Of all the aspects of the life of the apostle Peter, it is his friendship with Jesus that we see mostly clearly and in the most detail in the Gospels. We read of their very first meeting, after which it seems Peter seldom left Jesus' side. The tension that sometimes flares between the two, a tension which exists in any genuine and deep relationship, is seen again and again. Peter is the only one of Jesus' disciples we hear rebuking him, the only person who ever says no to him. Sometimes I wonder if Jesus didn't love him all the more for his passion. They were sometimes frustrated with each other, and yet they remained intimate friends.

APPLY: *What conflicts with friends do you need to resolve? How can conflict with a friend ultimately deepen your friendship?*

Leader Among the Twelve

With the help of Silas, whom I regard as a faithful brother,
I have written to you briefly, encouraging you and testifying
that this is the true grace of God. Stand fast in it.

1 PETER 5:12

It may make my Protestant friends uncomfortable if I make much of Peter and what I see as his unquestionable primacy. Peter was the first disciple to do practically everything, from preaching to healing. He was the leader among the Twelve. It may make my Catholic friends uncomfortable that although I make much of the primacy of Peter, I do not conclude that this leads to his supremacy. I am not interested in doing or undoing church history. But it seems clear to me that both Catholics and Protestants have missed Peter. I want to look for Simon Peter in the pages of the New Testament and seek to understand his emotional life.

JOURNAL: *What do you know about the personality of the apostle Peter? In what ways do you resemble him?*

The First Meeting

Andrew, Simon Peter's brother, was one of the two who heard what John had
said and who had followed Jesus. The first thing Andrew did was to find his brother
Simon and tell him, "We have found the Messiah" (that is, the Christ).
And he brought him to Jesus.

JOHN 1:40-42

Galilee was a good location for a small fishing business. This was the world of Simon and his brother Andrew. And so it was not in the high holy place of Jerusalem but in green and obscure Galilee that Jesus and Simon's life together began.

In the Gospel of John we have a record of their very first meeting. Andrew is curiously identified as Peter's brother, though we have not met Peter as yet. Andrew draws near with the same confession on his lips that his brother will later become famous for affirming. Standing there, seeing for the first time the man who will become his closest friend, Peter experiences the intent gaze of Jesus. John uses the same Greek word that Luke will later use to describe Jesus' piercing glance from across the high priest's courtyard when he hears Peter's final denial. But for now that scene is a world away.

PRAY: *If you had an "Andrew" who brought you to Christ, thank God for that person. Ask God to show you someone for whom you can be an "Andrew."*

"You Are ... You Will Be"

> *Jesus looked at him and said, "You are Simon son of John.*
> *You will be called Cephas" (which, when translated, is Peter).*

JOHN 1:42

We might imagine what Peter smelled like that morning, having fished all night. The pungent smell of the lake mixed with his sweat and the strong smell of fish—earthy, organic, common, repelling and somehow attracting all the same, like Simon himself. He was a simple fisherman, the son of a fisherman, with the most common given name of the day, *Simon*. The Greek *Peter* was not known before the second or third century. *Cephas,* the original Aramaic, was never known as a name.

Jesus takes a man with the most ordinary name in the land and gives him a new title. He will experience a future transformation not unlike that of Abraham, for in the Bible a new name signifies a new identity, a new life.

JOURNAL: *If Jesus gave you a new name based on what he wants you to become, what might it be? And why?*

A New Name

> *Jesus said to them, "Follow me and I will make you fish for people."*
> *And immediately they left their nets and followed him.*

MARK 1:17-18 NRSV

The understanding gaze of Jesus was not focused on the externals of the curious fisherman that morning. He looked into and saw the heart of who Simon was and what he would become. "You *are* Simon. . . . You *will be* called Cephas."

And so Simon sets out with the new title he has only begun to understand. Called away from his nets and boats, from his large comfortable home in Capernaum, from his wife and her mother, from the only life he has ever known, he is plunged into a life full of daily challenges, discomforts and surprises. In newfound obedience, Peter pushes out into a sea of humanity to catch men and women for God.

APPLY: *Into what unfamiliar "sea" of activity might God be calling you? What do you need to do in order to respond to that call?*

M O N D A Y   *Let Down the Nets*

> *When [Jesus] had finished speaking, he said to Simon,*
> *"Put out into deep water, and let down the nets for a catch."*
> *Simon answered, "Master, we've worked hard all night and haven't caught anything.*
> *But because you say so, I will let down the nets."*

LUKE 5:4-5

Jesus will never command the disciples to do something he has not first perfectly demonstrated in his own life. If he intends to call them to catch people, he will first show them how it is done. On this day it is Jesus who is fishing. He will cast his net and catch at least four: James, John, Andrew and, of course, Simon Peter.

Jesus begins by asking a favor. He asks to use one of their boats to give himself some room from the crush of the crowd and to keep from being pushed into the lake. Using a boat for a pulpit was an imaginative way to help the disciples begin to make the transition from being fishers of fish to fishers of people. How could they have known that they were washing their nets for perhaps the last time in their lives?

JOURNAL: *When has God surprised you with an unexpected change in your life? How did you respond?*

Fish Out of Nowhere

*When they had done so, they caught such a large
number of fish that their nets began to break.
So they signaled their partners in the other boat to come and help them,
and they came and filled both boats so full that they began to sink.
When Simon Peter saw this, he fell at Jesus' knees and said,
"Go away from me, Lord; I am a sinful man!"*

LUKE 5:6-8

It's as if the fish have appeared out of nowhere, as if they have been dropped into the nets from out of the blue Galilean sky. It's the kind of catch of which legends are made, a net-ripping catch! They call their partners to bring the other boat over and heave to. Even with their help the boats almost sink.

In response to the miraculous catch, Peter asks for what he really does not want—he asks for Jesus to leave. But what's so terrifying about a net full of fish? Even the miraculous fact that they had come from out of nowhere, out of a lake they knew was empty, is an occasion for wonder certainly, but fear?

PRAY: *When God gives us more than we prayed for, we usually don't know what to do. Pray that you will respond wisely when your prayers are answered in abundance.*

W E D N E S D A Y

Frightening Generosity

*For [Simon Peter] and all his companions were astonished at the catch of fish
they had taken, and so were James and John, the sons of Zebedee, Simon's partners.*

LUKE 5:9

Simon Peter has become the frightened fish, thrashing in the net, wanting only to get away, or at least for Jesus to get away from him. Thanks to the preaching of John the Baptist, Simon has become aware of his sinful state. And now he has become the beneficiary of Jesus, who has graciously filled his nets in spite of himself. There was nothing in his experience, nor in ours, that could have prepared him for this kind of frightening generosity. We are forever asking for the things we think we deserve. Simon knew then what we need to learn now: what we *deserve* is only death and separation from God and all his goodness.

JOURNAL: *Has God's generosity ever frightened you? What did it teach you about him and about yourself?*

The First to Confess

Repent, for the kingdom of heaven is near.

MATTHEW 3:2

Fear is what has driven Simon to his knees. He has heard the preaching of John the Baptist: "Repent, for the kingdom is at hand." Jesus' word is crucial: "Fear not!" Our sinfulness will ultimately be dealt with. Now, because of his coming, our sin can never stand between us and Jesus. Peter's confession of his sinfulness means he is precisely the man for whom Jesus is looking. In fact, he is the first person to confess his sinfulness to Jesus.

PRAY: *Offer the Lord what he longs to hear: the honest confession of your sin and your need for him.*

The Line in the Sand

Then Jesus said to Simon,
"Do not be afraid; from now on you will be catching people."

LUKE 5:10 NRSV

Jesus has come, and the line between the worlds of the Old Testament and the New is now clearly drawn in the sand beside the lake. The fishermen really have no choice. If they are to be faithful, they must follow. We too really have no choice. Waiting is no longer an option.

If we are honest, we'll admit that to follow, to really leave everything behind, is an absolutely terrifying prospect. Our most natural response would be, like Peter, to fall down and say, "Go away! This is more than I can deal with. I couldn't be the person you're looking for!"

APPLY: *What hinders you from following the Lord? What steps will you take to give it up for him?*

Let Go of the Nets

So they pulled their boats up on shore,
left everything and followed him.

LUKE 5:11

We stand before these terrifying possibilities, to let go of our security, to open ourselves to the frightening possibility of complete and utter success, to leave all that is familiar and safe for an unknown world.

Then we see that standing beside us is Jesus. He confidently whispers, "Don't be afraid. Let go of the nets. Do not be afraid. After all, it's me." Jesus has shown Simon that the sea he thought was empty was in fact full of fish. And Simon has begun to learn what it means to become partners with Jesus. A new kind of fishing lies ahead.

PRAY: *Commit yourself to Jesus, to become his partner in his kind of fishing.*

M O N D A Y *Choosing the Sinners*

After this, Jesus went out and saw a tax collector
by the name of Levi sitting at his tax booth.
"Follow me," Jesus said to him, and Levi got up,
left everything and followed him.

LUKE 5:27

Jesus does something mind-boggling to any observant Jew. As one of his first followers, Jesus calls Levi, or Matthew, the tax collector. Of the two types of tax collectors, Matthew was the most hated. He might have been in Capernaum collecting the fish tax, which would have led him into conflict with someone like Simon Peter.

In response to Jesus' call, Matthew gives a party at his own house. When the ever-present crowd of Pharisees object, Jesus responds that it is not the healthy who need a doctor, but the sick, and that he came to call not the righteous but sinners. I find it fascinating that Jesus does not reject the Pharisees' distinction between the "righteous" and the "sinners." It is only that, when given the choice, Jesus chooses the sinners!

APPLY: *Do you find yourself avoiding people who are classified as "sinners" from fear of what others might think? Make up your mind to find ways to include such people in your life. Remember that all of us are sinners whom Jesus loves.*

A Broken Jar

While he was in Bethany, reclining at
the table in the home of a man known as Simon the Leper,
a woman came in with an alabaster jar of very expensive perfume, made of pure nard.
She broke the jar and poured the perfume on his head.

MARK 14:3

No one noticed the woman at first. She slipped into the house in Bethany by a side entrance. In the middle of the meal she tiptoed to the place behind Jesus, who was reclining on his left elbow, Roman style. There she lingered for a moment. And then from the folds of her gown she produced a white alabaster jar. Moving to his side, without saying a word, she began to slowly pour the costly perfumed oil on his head. It ran down his forehead, dripping from both his eyebrows, wetting his lips and finally disappearing into his beard.

JOURNAL: *If you were present at the meal in Bethany, what would you think of the woman? How would you react to what she did?*

A Year's Wages "Wasted"

Some of those present were saying indignantly to one another,
"Why this waste of perfume? It could have been sold for more than a year's wages
and the money given to the poor." And they rebuked her harshly.

MARK 14:4-5

What the woman at Bethany did was creative. It was unexpected. And for some who watched, it was irritating. The disciples were angry at what seemed a great waste, a year's wages poured into the dust. They could have done something practical with the money, like feed the poor. As if such a tenderhearted and generous woman would have ever neglected the poor!

APPLY: *What gift can you give to the Lord which others would consider wasted on him? When and how will you give it?*

A Beautiful Thing

"Leave her alone," said Jesus.
"Why are you bothering her?
She has done a beautiful thing to me."

MARK 14 : 6

What the nameless woman did that evening created a space in time where the disciples could hear God—or not. But Jesus was the only person listening to the loving silence of what she had done. As they began to voice their disapproval, Jesus became indignant. "Leave her alone!" he said, wiping the perfume from his eyes. And then he spoke a word he seldom used, a word that is absolutely essential to our understanding of what creativity and art and the imagination are all about.

"Beautiful," he said. "What she has done to me is beautiful."

PRAY: *Pray that you will see the beauty in others' gifts for the Lord and that you will give lavishly, in the way he calls beautiful.*

"The Poor You Will Always Have with You"

The poor you will always have with you,
and you can help them any time you want.
But you will not always have me.
She did what she could.
She poured perfume on my body beforehand
to prepare for my burial.

MARK 14:7-8

The woman gave Jesus something infinitely more valuable than the perfume. She found a creative, imaginative way to give herself, to let Jesus know that he was loved and that he was not completely alone in being misunderstood. There was at least one other person who had heard what he said about dying soon. She had come to demonstrate her love while she could.

Like the woman, we have more to give than gifts. The greatest, most beautiful expression of our creativity is to find a way to give ourselves.

APPLY: *How can you give yourself in some unique and creative manner today? Look for some new and different way to give your presence, your time, your abilities or your means.*

She Did What She Could

I tell you the truth, wherever the gospel is preached throughout the world, what she has done will also be told, in memory of her.

MARK 14:9

Jesus makes a completely unique pronouncement over the nameless woman who anointed him at Bethany. This is the only record we have of his saying anything remotely like it. "Wherever the gospel is preached throughout the world, what she has done will also be told, in memory of her."

It is not the woman herself who is memorialized; it is what she did. But because of what she did, she will never be forgotten.

JOURNAL: *For what would you like to be remembered?*

MONDAY

When evening came, the boat was in the middle of the lake, and he was alone on land.
He saw the disciples straining at the oars, because the wind was against them.
About the fourth watch of the night he went out to them, walking on the lake.

MARK 6:47-48

Both Matthew and Mark tell us that Jesus had gone into the hills to pray. Only Mark's account (informed by Peter) gives us the detail that Jesus could see the disciples in their difficult situation. Both writers tell us Jesus left his prayers and walked on the water to be with his disciples. If they are caught in a struggle, he wants to be there with them.

Jesus walking on the sea is a divine revelation of who he is. He has just fed the five thousand. As the people received the bread, some of them began to murmur, "Could this be the prophet (like Moses)?" Although the disciples had missed the connection, at least some of the people in the crowd had begun to understand. Now Jesus walks on water. He is more than the manna provider; he is Deity.

JOURNAL: *When have you suddenly been aware that Christ was with you in a storm, that is, in a crisis which was beyond your abilities?*

The Call of Jesus

"Lord, if it's you," Peter replied, "tell me to come to you on the water."
"Come," he said.

MATTHEW 14:28-29

What sort of person wants to walk on the water in the middle of a dark windstorm? Was Peter motivated by some innate desire to do what he saw Jesus doing? Or did he want to walk on the water simply so he could be with Jesus? Whatever the reason, Peter's peculiarly worded question shows that he is beginning to understand that only the call of Jesus will make the impossibility of walking on the water possible.

With all that he doesn't know, Simon somehow does understand that the call must originate with Jesus. This explains the clumsy wording of his request. "If it's you, tell me to come to you," he shouts above the howling wind. Bonhoeffer says that discipleship is never an offer we make to Christ. It is only the call of Jesus that makes everything possible.

APPLY: *How have you sensed the call of Jesus on your life in the past? How do you sense it now? What do you feel he wants you to do next in dependence on him?*

Then Peter got out of the boat, walked on the water and came toward Jesus.
But when he saw the wind, he was afraid and, beginning to sink, cried out, "Lord, save me!"
Immediately Jesus reached out his hand and caught him.
"You of little faith," he said, "why did you doubt?"

MATTHEW 14:29-31

Was Peter's request courage or insanity or a little bit of both? In fact Peter's short walk was indeed a triumph of faith. It was his first miracle!

But then the experiment went terribly wrong. Peter looked around at reality and began to do what he should have done naturally: he began to sink. In the midst of the miracle he doubted the new reality he had just stepped into. He apparently had no doubt when he stepped out on the water. He asked for no proof beyond Jesus' command to come to him. When he saw the wild waves, however, he began to need proof that the impossible could somehow be possible.

There is no proof great enough to prevent doubt. If you base your belief on proof, sooner or later you will sink. Notice that Peter does not say, "If you can save me." He just yells, "Save me!" Peter finds Jesus' hand is immediately there, saving him, holding him up.

PRAY: *Right now do you need to pray, "Lord, save me"? If not right now, you will feel that way some time soon. Reach out and let the hand of Jesus grasp you and pull you to safety.*

> But ask in faith, never doubting,
> for the one who doubts is like a wave of the sea,
> driven and tossed by the wind.

JAMES 1:6 NRSV

Why did Peter doubt? He had begun to accomplish what he set out to do; he had walked on the water. But there was a deeper lesson he had to learn, and Jesus was intent on him not missing it. You and I must also learn it if we are to move forward through the windstorm of following Jesus.

The lesson is that Peter needed to sink in order to take the next step of faith in Jesus. Walking on the water does not ultimately increase our faith; only sinking does! Those who ask for miracles and receive them soon forget. But those who suffer for Christ's sake never forget. They have their own wounds to remind them.

JOURNAL: *How have you learned through failure?*

You Are the Son of God!

And when they climbed into the boat, the wind died down.
Then those who were in the boat worshiped him,
saying, "Truly you are the Son of God."

MATTHEW 14:32-33

Jesus and the half-soaked Peter climb into the boat, and the wind, as if exhausted as well, dies down. And then something even more extraordinary occurs. At the previous storm the disciples wondered, "Who is this man?" Now they have begun to know. We have never heard or seen the disciples worshiping him until this moment. "Truly you are the Son of God!" they confess.

Mark, in his account, does not tell us about their worship. He speaks of their complete amazement over Jesus. He looks back at the feeding of the five thousand and tells us that the disciples had not understood about the loaves because of the hardness of their hearts. Not until they saw Jesus walking on the water did they put it all together. The feeding and the walking on water were both crucial manifestations of the true nature of Jesus, of his oneness with the Father. When the disciples finally understood, they worshiped him.

JOURNAL: *When and how did you move from wondering "Who is this man?" to worshiping Jesus as the Son of God?*

His divine power has given us everything we need for life and godliness
through our knowledge of him who called us by his own glory and goodness.

2 PETER 1:3

Jesus will never condemn Peter, or us, for looking at reality. The waves and the wind are real. But Jesus calls to Peter, and to you and me, to look beyond all that, to a new reality where walking on the water is also real, and so is feeding thousands of people with a few crumbs, and rising from the dead.

The world has a million confusing faces: our fragile health, hunger, our fallen situation, aching loneliness. The world Jesus calls us into has one focus: him! When Peter looks only at the face of Jesus, he begins to rise toward that new world, the world of the kingdom. There is one certain way to know if you've had a brush with that other impossible new world. You will find yourself doing what the disciples did when they got Jesus back into their boat: you will find yourself worshiping him.

PRAY: *Thank the Lord that you are part of his new reality. Commit to him all the seemingly impossible obstacles and problems of your life.*

M O N D A Y

Jesus' True Nature

After six days Jesus took with him Peter, James and John the brother of James,
and led them up a high mountain by themselves.
There he was transfigured before them.
His face shone like the sun, and his clothes became as white as the light.

MATTHEW 17:1-2

The account of the transfiguration comes and goes like a flash, like the burst of light that was Jesus' transfigured face. This is not a transformation; that is, Jesus does not change his form. Rather, the three disciples are allowed to see Jesus' true nature, as he has been all along, only their eyes have just now been opened. The veil is lifted for a few precious minutes.

The experience was absolutely a defining moment for Simon. Jesus is transfigured. But Peter is transformed! The sight of Jesus in his true glory confirms that Peter's earlier confession was true. Jesus is the Messiah! He is the glorious Son of the living God.

JOURNAL: *If you had been there on the mountain of transfiguration, what do you think would have been the most frightening part of the experience? the most amazing part of the experience?*

Unveiled Glory

> *As he was praying, the appearance of his face changed,*
> *and his clothes became as bright as a flash of lightning.*
> *Two men, Moses and Elijah, appeared in glorious splendor, talking with Jesus.*
> *They spoke about his departure, which he was about to bring to fulfillment at Jerusalem.*

L U K E   9 : 2 9 - 3 1

Only Luke, with his emphasis on prayer, tells us that the transfiguration was a response to Jesus' prayer. His countenance as well as his clothing became as bright as light itself. What Peter, James and John witnessed was nothing less than unveiled glory. This is who Jesus has been all along.

All at once they saw that Jesus was no longer alone. There was no explanation of how the three recognized Moses and Elijah; nevertheless, they were aware that they were suddenly in the presence of two of the greatest figures of the Old Testament. Only Luke tells us what they were discussing with Jesus. He uses the word *exodus*. They were talking about Jesus' upcoming exodus at Jerusalem.

Paul speaks of "the light of the knowledge of the glory of God in the face of Christ" (2 Corinthians 4:6). That knowledge, that Truth, is now blazing before Peter, James and John.

PRAY: *The One who was joined by Moses and Elijah on that mountain is with you today. What will you say to him? What is he saying to you?*

Terrified by Glory

> *Peter said to Jesus, "Rabbi, it is good for us to be here.*
> *Let us put up three shelters—one for you, one for Moses and one for Elijah."*
> *(He did not know what to say, they were so frightened.)*

MARK 9:5-6

Often in the presence of Peter, when Jesus reveals his true nature in a new way, the first words from his lips are "Don't be afraid." When the nets miraculously fill with fish, when he calms the storm, when he walks on the water, when he is transfigured into blazing light and when he is raised from the dead—each time Jesus comforts and calms Peter with these words.

In each instance, when the veil is momentarily lifted and Peter has the terrifying realization that he, a veteran sinner, is in the presence of undiminished Deity, it totally undoes him (as indeed it should). Have you ever come close enough to be terrified by the glory of Jesus?

APPLY: *In worship do you ever take the Lord's presence too casually? How can you introduce a greater sense of awe into your worship? Remember that Jesus also says, "Don't be afraid."*

> *I tell you the truth, some who are standing here will not taste death*
> *before they see the kingdom of God come with power.*

MARK 9:1

Jesus' transfiguration will become the most powerful revelation of his glory that any of the disciples will ever see. When they witness the cross, all they will see is a man being tortured to death. The resurrection will not be witnessed by anyone except two angels. The moment of transfiguration will be the only revelation of the true nature of Jesus' glory until the *parousia*—his coming again in clouds of glory.

Six days earlier, Jesus had made a fantastic promise to the disciples: that some of them would live to see the kingdom of God arrive. Though there are other interpretations of Jesus' statement, I believe this transcendent experience on the mountain is the fulfillment of that enigmatic promise to Peter, James and John.

JOURNAL: *Have you ever wished to see Christ in his glory? Do you think the experience would be joyful, terrifying, overwhelming, dumbfounding, or some other adjective? Why do you think he does not reveal himself to us in that way?*

A Glimpse of Heaven

While he was still speaking, a bright cloud enveloped them,
and a voice from the cloud said,
"This is my Son, whom I love; with him I am well pleased. Listen to him!"
When the disciples heard this, they fell facedown to the ground, terrified.

MATTHEW 17:5-6

God provides a cloud to envelop and afford the disciples the protection they want but no longer need. The cloud is said to have *overshadowed* them. This is the same word that was used of the Spirit of God *overshadowing* Mary at the moment of the incarnation. Perhaps now the potential for a new understanding can be born in the hearts of the disciples. The voice Jesus heard at his baptism, at the inauguration of his ministry, is heard once more as he nears its completion, as he makes ready for his exodus.

On that mountain the three disciples got a glimpse into heaven. They discovered that not all mysteries will be explained there, but instead we will know how truly vast and unknowable the mystery of Christ is.

PRAY: *Pray about any mysteries which trouble you—those things about Christ and his workings which you don't understand. Ask for the courage to leave those unknowns with him.*

"Don't Be Afraid"

Jesus came and touched them. "Get up," he said.
"Don't be afraid." When they looked up, they saw no one except Jesus.

MATTHEW 17:7-8

Having fallen to the ground in terror a moment before, the disciples look up and see only Jesus. He is himself once more, ordinary. He touches each of them on the shoulder. "Don't be afraid," he says.

Whenever he is revealed to them, those are always the first words on his lips. When the nets were miraculously filled, he looked down at the kneeling Peter and said, "Don't be afraid; from now on you'll catch people." When he calmed the demonic storm on the sea he asked, "Why were you afraid?" As he approached their boat, walking on the water, he called out, "I am, don't be afraid." And now as the terror is draining from their faces he speaks those same comforting words. When later he is raised from the dead, he will speak them to the women at the tomb: "Don't be afraid."

JOURNAL: *How have revelation and terror been linked in your experience? How has Jesus reassured you, "Don't be afraid"?*

M O N D A Y *The Hand of Acceptance*

Accept one another, then, just as Christ accepted you,
in order to bring praise to God.

ROMANS 15:7

First Missionary Baptist Church was all black. When I visited, I was the only white person in the sanctuary. I sat in the back in the only empty seat I could find. I was nervous. Several people around me felt the same way.

As the sermon began, the elderly woman next to me took my hand in hers. At first I didn't know what to do, so I did nothing at all. Every time the preacher would make a point, she would give my hand a squeeze. She was unaware of what she was doing. I learned later that she and her husband Bob had raised over forty foster children. Dinah quite simply is a magnet who draws to herself people to love. Whenever she is asked why she adopted so many children, she responds, "Who else is going to love them if not me?"

That Sunday morning I became part of Dinah's extended family. With the reach of her hand I was accepted as well.

APPLY: *Ask yourself the question, "Who else is going to love them if not me?" Who comes to mind as "them"?*

> *At Caesarea there was a man named Cornelius,*
> *a centurion in what was known as the Italian Regiment.*
> *He and all his family were devout and God-fearing;*
> *he gave generously to those in need and prayed to God regularly.*

ACTS 10:1-2

For almost fifteen years Christianity had existed solely as a sect within Judaism. Its center of faith was still the temple in Jerusalem. There were still those in leadership in the church who desired that things stay that way. With the outreach to the Samaritans, tension had begun to build. Now matters will come to a point of crisis.

The incident takes place deep in enemy territory. Caesarea was the Roman capital of Judea. The fact that Cornelius, the object of the story, is a high-ranking Roman officer makes matters even worse. He represents all that is loathsome to the Jews. But then again he is devout. The term *God-fearer* indicates that he is a Gentile who worshiped the God of Israel but would not become a full proselyte. Still he is a hated Roman and an unclean Gentile. Despite Cornelius's affinity for Judaism, no observant Jew would have shared a meal with him, nor even entered his house. It is important to note that God sent a vision to both Cornelius and Peter to help prepare them for their life-changing experiences.

JOURNAL: *Who are some surprising believers you know, people whom you would not expect to come to faith in Christ?*

> *[Peter] went in and found that many had assembled; and he said to them,*
> *"You yourselves know that it is unlawful for a Jew to associate with or to visit a Gentile;*
> *but God has shown me that I should not call anyone profane or unclean."*

ACTS 10:27-28 NRSV

Jesus can make anyone clean, even the last person on earth Peter would expect to be clean: a Roman soldier, one of the very ones who had crucified Jesus. What an earthquake in Peter's soul! It was a direct assault on his most basic beliefs. But Jesus had come to shatter and redefine everything. Certainly it is a shattered Simon who makes his way, for the first time in his life, into a Gentile dwelling. He will find there men and women like himself who want nothing less than to eat the true bread of heaven. People who, though they live in darkness, have nonetheless seen a great Light!

The crowd Peter would have crossed the street to avoid, would have denied meal fellowship with, seems now bathed in a new light. He sees bright eyes and hungry faces. He looks out at men and women, boys and girls who will suffer every bit as much as he will in the years to come for their allegiance to Jesus. He looks out on brothers and sisters.

APPLY: *In your opinion who are the least likely candidates for faith in Christ? What can you and your church do to extend yourselves to them for the Lord?*

Holy Spirit Interruption

Then Peter said, "Can anyone keep these people from being baptized with water?
They have received the Holy Spirit just as we have."

ACTS 10:46

Peter will not even make it through his sermon before the Holy Spirit, who so longs to embrace all men and women, will interrupt him and pour himself out on them all. Peter does not even have a chance to lay hands on them. This is completely a work of God, Peter realizes. It is a lesson he will carry with him all his life.

From this point on, true leadership in the church will be exercised only by those who are willing to listen to the Spirit. Only those who are able to embrace and preserve the universal vision that Peter glimpsed there in the house of Cornelius will be fit shepherds. The task will never again be a matter of guarding the old orthodoxy. From this day on it will be new wine in new wineskins.

APPLY: *What are your church's standards for leadership? How do they compare with the standards expressed here?*

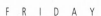

If Not Us, Who?

> *We believe it is through the grace of our Lord Jesus Christ*
> *that we are saved, just as they are.*

ACTS 15:11

Peter, the unquestioned leader of the church until this time, now virtually disappears into the mission field. He disappears into a sea of so-called unclean Gentiles. Even as Jesus chose to let go of power and authority, so Peter lets go as well. He never forgot the lesson in the upper room, that true greatness involves taking up the basin and the towel. He would wash feet with the water of Jesus' word for the remainder of his life.

There are a thousand ways to wash feet. It might take the form of a cup of cold water offered in Jesus' name. Perhaps it might be a simple touch on the shoulder. For Peter it was the willingness to go someplace he knew he was not supposed to be in obedience to Jesus' call, to cross a line no one had ever crossed before.

JOURNAL: *Whose feet will you wash today and in the days to come, and how?*

Then Peter began to speak to them:
"I truly understand that God shows no partiality, but in every nation
anyone who fears him and does what is right is acceptable to him."

ACTS 10:34-35 NRSV

Though it has been years, I still have not found my way completely into the congregation of First Missionary Baptist, though I am always more than welcomed. Some lines take years to cross. I can only tell you that my awkward attempt at racial reconciliation is a response to a fragmented part of my life, a piece of a puzzle that may never fully come together. All I know is that something in me longs to find a place for it to fit.

There comes a moment in our lives when some of the pieces of the puzzle come together, where all our past experiences, both good and bad, are brought to bear in causing us to become who God intends us to be. The encounter of Cornelius was just such a moment in Peter's life. Everything that had happened to him up until that time came together in the crucible of that moment, causing him to respond in just the way he did. As a result of his reluctant obedience, he was never the same.

PRAY: *Ask God to show you any ways in which you show partiality, especially in your attitudes toward other Christians. Pray for a more open heart.*

M O N D A Y

Precision and Patience

> *Humble yourselves, therefore, under God's mighty hand,*
> *that he may lift you up in due time.*

1 PETER 5:6

Paul's greatest strength was also his greatest weakness. He had brought into the new faith his pharisaic presets. Among those the most prominent was the desire to "get it right." You might call it theological exactitude.

Peter's presets were totally different. They were more agrarian. He brought with him the concern to be in the right place, to use the right bait, whether to catch fish or people. He was more patient. Though Paul had known brokenness, it was not to the degree Peter had known it.

We need the passion for correctness that we find in Paul. But we also need the stable bridge of Peter to continue to help us cross over.

APPLY: *Do you tend toward Paul's desire to get things right or Peter's desire to be a reconciler? How can you move toward the direction where you are lacking?*

> *But you are a chosen people, a royal priesthood,*
> *a holy nation, a people belonging to God,*
> *that you may declare the praises of him*
> *who called you out of darkness into his wonderful light.*
> *Once you were not a people, but now you are the people of God;*
> *once you had not received mercy, but now you have received mercy.*

1 PETER 2:9-10

Over their two and a half to three years together, Jesus and Peter became the truest of friends. True friends define each other, as we see most clearly in Peter's Caesarea Philippi confession.

"Who am I?" Jesus asked.

"You are the Christ," Peter responded.

"You are the Rock," Jesus completed the exchange.

Sometime before A.D. 65, Peter wrote two letters to a mixed group of Gentile and Jewish Christians, an appropriate flock for a shepherd who had sacrificed so much to bring the two together. In his letters Peter defines us; he tells us who we are. We are pilgrims and strangers; we are newborn babies and obedient children; we are free slaves of God, an elect race, a royal priesthood, a holy nation, God's own possession. We are the flock of God.

JOURNAL: *Consider the word-pictures Peter uses for believers in 1 Peter 2:9-10. Which one speaks to you most deeply, and why?*

A Poignant Farewell

Finally, all of you, have unity of spirit, sympathy, love for one another,
a tender heart, and a humble mind.
Do not repay evil or abuse for abuse; but, on the contrary, repay with a blessing.
It is for this that you were called—that you might inherit a blessing.

1 PETER 3:8-9 NRSV

Peter's letters represent a poignant farewell. Jesus had earlier told him about the manner of his death and had strongly hinted that it would entail crucifixion (John 21:18). Now Peter has been given to understand that his own "exodus" is near. So, remarkably, we have in the letters, especially the second letter, his last will and testament. He is clearly burdened by the threat of false teachers who have infiltrated the churches. He will encapsulate his last spiritual advice in two passages. In the first, 1 Peter 3:8-9, he condenses his admonition to five simple imperatives: live in harmony, be sympathetic, love deeply, be compassionate and humble, and bless those who do you evil. His advice might also be a sketch of his spiritual life, of all that Jesus has accomplished in his own spirit over the years.

PRAY: *Pray 1 Peter 3:8-9 for yourself: that you will live in harmony with fellow believers, be sympathetic, love deeply, be compassionate and humble, and bless those who do you evil.*

> For this reason, make every effort to add to your faith goodness;
> and to goodness, knowledge; and to knowledge, self-control;
> and to self-control, perseverance; and to perseverance, godliness;
> and to godliness, brotherly kindness; and to brotherly kindness, love.

2 PETER 1:5-7

The statement has been rightly called the Ladder of Faith, for each concept builds on the former. The bookends of this remarkable statement are *faith* and *love*. They might be the bookends of Peter's own spiritual journey. What began with a statement of faith at Caesarea Philippi ended in a missionary life defined and dominated by love.

This amazing pillar, the Rock, perhaps the last living link to Jesus besides John, simply and humbly identifies himself as a *fellow elder* (1 Peter 5:1). He has poured out his life trying to obey Jesus' final admonition to feed and care for his sheep. He has lost everything for the sake of the call: his possessions, his authority. As he looks his own death squarely in the face, he fearlessly thinks only of the fate of the little flock he will leave behind. And he writes for them and for us two precious letters.

APPLY: *Realizing that the steps are not necessarily chronological, where do you place yourself on the "ladder of faith" in 2 Peter 1:5-7?*

The Foundational Disciple

As you come to him, the living Stone—
rejected by men but chosen by God and precious to him—you also, like living stones,
are being built into a spiritual house to be a holy priesthood,
offering spiritual sacrifices acceptable to God through Jesus Christ.

1 PETER 2:4-5

From simple fisherman to struggling disciple to first confessor, from despairing denier to fearless leader, from ambitious go-getter to humble servant. The progression goes something like that. It is miraculous that Jesus chose someone like Peter, whom we all identify with in one way or another, a person who teaches us more through his weaknesses than his strengths.

Peter humbly turns the title *Rock*, which eventually became his true name, into an invitation. In his eyes we are all supposed to be living stones. But without a doubt he was the first of these stones to be laid, the foundational disciple. The pride that led him at first to join in the debates about who was the greatest was definitively defeated in the course of his walk with Jesus.

JOURNAL: *In your own life how has the Lord dealt with pride? What further work would you like him to do in that area?*

The Power to Let Go

See, I lay a stone in Zion,
a chosen and precious cornerstone,
and the one who trusts in him
will never be put to shame.

1 PETER 2:6

We need to gain from Peter's example the power to let go—to let go of possessions and power, to let go of position and authority, to give in at last, as he finally did, to the service of the basin and the towel with all its bitter consequences. If we are to be living stones, if the church is to go on being built the way Jesus desires it to be built, then Peter's story must in some sense become our story. Only then will our story become like Peter's, the story of Jesus.

Hear again Peter's gracious invitation to join him in becoming living stones: Come to Christ, who is the living cornerstone of God's temple. He was rejected by the people, but he is precious to God who chose him. And God is building us, as living stones, into his spiritual temple.

PRAY: *Thank God that you are included in his spiritual temple. Pray that you will do your part as a living stone.*

MONDAY

What Have You Left Behind?

> *None of you can become my disciple*
> *if you do not give up all your possessions.*

LUKE 14:33 NRSV

I am not a prophet, but I do have one reoccurring vision. I see a path disappearing in the distance. Either side is strewn with various objects. A cloak. A cane. An expensive car, the door left open, the keys still in the ignition. The objects represent things people have left to follow Jesus. In the vision I keep looking for things I have left behind for his sake.

Almost everyone who follows Jesus in the New Testament leaves something behind. Simon and the other disciples who were fishermen left their nets and boats. James and John, the sons of Zebedee, left their father as well as a prosperous family business. Matthew left behind an even more lucrative business, tax gathering. The woman at the well ran off and forgot her water jar. The sinful woman left behind an empty alabaster perfume jar. Lazarus, perhaps the most miraculous of all, left behind a pile of grave clothes and an empty tomb.

APPLY: *What have you left behind in order to follow Christ? What do you think you still need to discard?*

He Gives Us Himself

No one can serve two masters;
for a slave will either hate the one and love the other,
or be devoted to the one and despise the other.
You cannot serve God and wealth.

MATTHEW 6:24 NRSV

The farther down you get on the path of objects discarded for Jesus' sake, the higher the possessions piled on either side. With each object the travelers also leave behind a small piece of themselves, because a possession isn't a little something you own, as much as something that owns a little bit of you. We leave behind a part of our old self.

In return for whatever small thing we discard, Jesus gives us a part of himself in exchange. With him is great freedom from those things we leave behind, freedom from that greatest self-possessing possession, our "self."

JOURNAL: *Consider what you have discarded for Christ. How has the act of leaving things behind led to freedom for you? How has Christ compensated you with his blessings, especially his own presence?*

Tear Up the Roof

When Jesus saw their faith, he said to the paralytic,
"Son, your sins are forgiven."

MARK 2:5

So many people were present to hear Jesus speak that the paralytic and his friends couldn't get to the door of the house. So the paralytic's friends climbed up on the roof, dismantled the tiles and lowered the man into the house. Picture the lesson being interrupted by someone being lowered from the ceiling! I can imagine a smile of amusement on Jesus' face at the sight of such faith. The man would allow nothing to keep him from Jesus—not the roof, not his paralysis, not even fear of the crowd. In response to his faith, Jesus forgave his sins and healed him.

Make the decision now that nothing will separate you from his love, whether it is something as flimsy as a dollar bill or as hard as a tile roof.

PRAY: *Ask the Holy Spirit to show you anything that stands between you and Jesus. It could be a material desire, a hurt you refuse to forgive or a sin you need to confess. Then take steps today to remove that obstacle.*

A Way to Give Ourselves

Jesus looked at him and loved him.
"One thing you lack," he said. "Go, sell everything you have and give to the poor,
and you will have treasure in heaven. Then come, follow me."

MARK 10:21

Whenever Jesus talked about money, he had to ask for some as an example or obtain it in some miraculous way. Jesus was penniless. Yet he instructed the rich young ruler to give away everything, knowing that his money was standing between him and total obedience to God. Jesus apparently asked the disciples to do the same thing, for at one point Peter responded, "Lord, we have left everything in order to follow you."

Jesus never tells us to do something he has not perfectly lived out. So why would he encourage people to give money to the poor when he never did so himself? Isn't it simply because he had no money to give them? So what did Jesus give to the poor? The answer is, of course, he gave them himself.

JOURNAL: *In addition to giving money to those who have less than you have, how can you give yourself, so that Christ can give himself through you?*

Impossible Commands

They were greatly astounded and said to one another,
"Then who can be saved?"
Jesus looked at them and said, "For mortals it is impossible, but not for God;
for God all things are possible."

MARK 10:26-27 NRSV

Everything is upside down in Jesus' new domain. It is the poor, hungry, weeping ones who are blessed, while the rich and well-fed are given warning. It is a world dominated by enemy-love, radical acceptance of others and overflowing hearts. It is a world to which none of us can possibly hope to aspire. When the rich man turns away from Jesus, just before Jesus enters Jerusalem for the Passion, it is in response to another of those impossible commands, to sell everything and give it away to the poor. As the dejected man walks away, Jesus remarks how difficult it is for the rich to enter the Kingdom. This statement unsettles the Twelve, who have been raised to see wealth as an unqualified blessing from God. And then it comes, the perfect words of Jesus, that what is impossible for human beings is possible with God. Jesus awakens in us a fresh realization of our need for him by means of his impossible commands.

APPLY: *Which of Christ's commands seems least possible for you to carry out? Rather than turn away or ignore the command, let it lead you to depend on him completely.*

Make a Place for Prayer

Then he entered the temple area and began driving out those who were selling.
"It is written," he said to them, "'My house will be a house of prayer';
but you have made it 'a den of robbers.'"

LUKE 19:45-46

The merchants had set up their booths in the Court of the Gentiles, a place reserved for prayer for non-Jewish believers or *God-fearers,* of whom there were many. A low wall separated it from the inner courts, which were reserved for Jews only. The court where the merchants had set up shop was the only place for Gentiles to offer prayers of thanksgiving and praise to God. Now, with the clamor of the merchants going on all around, they had no place to be alone with the Lord.

"My house will be called a house of prayer," Jesus thundered at the merchants. He was as upset about the Gentiles not having a place to pray as he was with the commercialism of the merchants.

Jesus' voice also speaks to me: "Make a place for those who long to speak to me. Do absolutely nothing to hinder them and absolutely everything to help them, even if you must turn over a few tables in the process."

JOURNAL: *How have you observed contemporary Christians hindering people who long to speak to Jesus?*

MONDAY   *Amazed by Authority*

> *When Jesus had finished saying these things,*
> *the crowds were amazed at his teaching,*
> *because he taught as one who had authority,*
> *and not as their teachers of the law.*

MATTHEW 7:28-29

The people were amazed by the authority and freshness of Jesus' preaching. He did not teach like the rabbis, whose erudition was demonstrated by the list of rabbinic sayings they could quote on any of an impressive number of subjects. No, Jesus simply spoke the truth. If he quoted anyone it was God himself.

When the authorities would later hear the formally uneducated Peter and his companions preach, and they would recall the passion and authority they had heard only once before from the Nazarene, the authorities would remember that these men had "been with Jesus" (Acts 4:13).

PRAY: *Pray that people will recognize daily that you have been with Jesus.*

Creation Obeys

The disciples went and woke him, saying,
"Master, Master, we're going to drown!"
He got up and rebuked the wind and the raging waters;
the storm subsided, and all was calm.

LUKE 8 : 24

There were times when creation recognized the authority of Jesus. At least once he spoke to the winds. "Be quiet!" he said, in the way you or I might speak to our dog, and they obeyed. To the waves he said, "Calm down!" and they too obeyed. The disciples were terrified. "Who is this?" they stammered in fear. "Even the wind and the waves obey him!"

I sometimes ask myself if I might have felt safer that day in the water, rather than in the boat with someone who possessed such awesome power. When Jesus desired, he could lift the veil of his incarnation and speak in such a way that creation could recognize him for who he was.

JOURNAL: *Place yourself in the boat with Jesus and the disciples. He has just rebuked the storm, and all is quiet. What do you think? How do you react?*

An Unorthodox Presence

Everyone was amazed and gave praise to God.
They were filled with awe and said,
"We have seen remarkable things today."

LUKE 5:26

After healing a paralyzed man (whose friends had torn a hole in the roof!) Jesus confronts the Pharisees with the question of which is easier to say, "Your sins are forgiven" or "Get up and walk." The answer? Both are humanly impossible. It is a matter of authority, Jesus says. And he has it!

The end of the story is unique in the New Testament. The people respond, "We have seen *remarkable* things today." The word is *paradoxon* and it is found nowhere else in the Bible. From it we get our word *paradox*. Literally it means *contrary* (*para*) to what would otherwise bring *glory* (*doxa*). (This is my rendering.)

The Gospels portray Jesus as an unorthodox presence in the context of first-century Judaism. His presence is still challenging our ideas of what is religiously correct.

JOURNAL: *How have you found Jesus to be remarkable? How has he challenged your religious ideas?*

A Surprising Faith

A centurion's servant, whom his master valued highly, was sick and about to die.
The centurion heard of Jesus and sent some elders of the Jews to him,
asking him to come and heal his servant.
When they came to Jesus, they pleaded earnestly with him,
"This man deserves to have you do this, because he loves our nation
and has built our synagogue." So Jesus went with them.

LUKE 7:2-6

Jesus has entered the town of Capernaum. The nameless soldier had heard about the healings Jesus had done there earlier. Now one of the centurion's slaves is gravely ill, and he cares enough to send for Jesus. The centurion is a *God-fearer*, a Gentile who worshiped the God of Israel but would not submit to ritual circumcision. The centurion loves the Jews, whom the culture says he should hate. He cares for a lowly slave. Though he represents the power of Rome, he is humble. Throughout Jesus' life, Pharisees and legal professionals will test and try him to the limit, while tax collectors, prostitutes and Gentiles will display a faith never seen in Israel.

APPLY: *Whose faith surprises you? What can you learn from that person?*

The Answer I Don't Deserve

The centurion sent friends to say to [Jesus]:
"Lord, don't trouble yourself, for I do not deserve to have you come under my roof.
That is why I did not even consider myself worthy to come to you.
But say the word, and my servant will be healed."

LUKE 7:6-7

The centurion's Jewish friends had insisted that he *deserved* to have Jesus heal his servant. But then the centurion sends a very different message. "I *don't* deserve this," he says. Nevertheless, he still expects and requests Jesus to heal his servant. In the process, miraculously, it is Jesus who is amazed.

So, what was it that amazed Jesus? The fact that the Gentile soldier had begun to live out Jesus' unorthodox command to love his enemies, the Jews? The fact that this powerful man attributed to Jesus a greater power and authority? Or was Jesus amazed that the soldier possessed a faith that still did not exist anywhere in Israel? He asked for what he knew he *didn't* deserve and faithfully expected to get it anyway!

JOURNAL: *Have you ever secretly felt that you deserved an answer to your prayers? How does the centurion's story affect you?*

Unworthy but Bold

I myself am a man under authority, with soldiers under me.
I tell this one, "Go," and he goes; and that one, "Come," and he comes.
I say to my servant, "Do this," and he does it.

LUKE 7:8

The centurion acknowledges that he is not worthy of a visit from the rabbi from Nazareth. He is a soldier, acquainted with the rigors of the Roman military. He would have been prepared to fall on his own sword at the command of his superior officer. He understands authority, and he recognizes that Jesus possesses a vast authority.

Jesus utters not a single word of healing. He only marvels at the faith of the Gentile God-fearer. Without even being present in the home that was "not worthy" for him to enter, without a word Jesus heals the servant.

PRAY: *Do not ask for what you think you deserve, for none of us is deserving. Boldly ask the Lord for what you need today, understanding that he has the authority to answer your request.*

M O N D A Y

Different Kinds of Stars

Do everything without complaining or arguing,
so that you may become blameless and pure,
children of God without fault in a crooked and depraved generation,
in which you shine like stars in the universe as you hold out the word of life.

PHILIPPIANS 2:14-16

We describe some people as *stars*. We look up to them, at their apparent brilliance, and feel ourselves small and insignificant by comparison. They move across the sky of life, luminaries attracting most of the attention and admiration. Like the moon they constantly change their faces to suit the season. Like the sun they often burn hot. Like meteors they usually burn up quickly.

JOURNAL: *Do you tend to be attracted to people who are stars in the eyes of the world? How can their example be misleading, even deceptive?*

North Star People

Those who are wise will shine like the brightness of the heavens,
and those who lead many to righteousness, like the stars for ever and ever.

DANIEL 12:3

When sailors or even astronauts are lost, they look for Polaris, the North Star, to regain their sense of direction. Polaris is a dim, slightly green star, always in the same spot, the tip of the northern axis that goes through the celestial sphere. It takes a bit of time to learn to find it. People who have it pointed out to them for the first time usually say, "Oh, is that the North Star? I thought it would be brighter."

I want to campaign for the idea of our becoming North Star people. We might not seem as bright or as interesting as some. Seldom will people point their telescopes at us. When they do, they will no doubt respond, "Oh, I thought she was brighter than that." But as North Star people we can serve a deeper purpose. When people need us, we can be there for them, pointing the Way. While the world is spinning at a dizzying pace, we can remain grounded to the same spot, less dazzling but unmovable.

APPLY: *Who has been a North Star person for you? How can you imitate that person?*

Turn to His Light

> *He had no beauty or majesty to attract us to him,*
> *nothing in his appearance that we should desire him.*

ISAIAH 53:2

Jesus was a North Star person. According to Isaiah there was nothing in his appearance that seemed especially brilliant. In his time there were far more dazzling messianic stars who came and went with a flash. But Jesus has always remained there, rooted to the same place in the universe, unmovable. He constantly calls out to us to turn around and behold the dazzling dimness of his light, as it shines in this present world—to find our way to it, and then to find our way by it.

PRAY: *Pray that you will stay focused on Jesus, the unchanging and unmovable North Star.*

Which Way Preserves Life?

[Jesus] went into the synagogue, and a man with a shriveled hand was there.
Some of them were looking for a reason to accuse Jesus, so they watched him closely to see
if he would heal him on the Sabbath. Jesus said to the man with the shriveled hand,
"Stand up in front of everyone." Then Jesus asked them, "Which is lawful on the Sabbath:
to do good or to do evil, to save life or to kill?" But they remained silent.

MARK 3:1-4

It is the Sabbath, and Jesus appears once more in the synagogue. He has become so notorious for breaking the Pharisees' oral additions to the biblical limitations of the Sabbath that the Pharisees are uneasy, expecting him to defy them.

The rabbis had agreed upon a single precept to help them deal with exceptions to the Sabbath. Whenever there was a conflict of observance, the single deciding question was, "Which way preserves life?" The rabbi from Nazareth quotes their own teaching to them as he calls the man with the deformed hand to stand in front of the congregation. Normally such a confrontation would lead to a debate, but such debate is useless in the authority of the presence of Jesus. He is angered *by* them and yet grieving *for* them at the same time.

JOURNAL: *Consider a conflict in which you are now engaged. Which way preserves life? Which way is closer to the character of Jesus?*

"Stretch Out Your Hand"

> *He looked around at them in anger and, deeply distressed at their stubborn hearts,*
> *said to the man, "Stretch out your hand."*
> *He stretched it out, and his hand was completely restored.*

MARK 3:5

Jesus gives the simple command, "Stretch out your hand." No thunder is heard in the distance, no one is blinded by a flash of light, and yet the perfect intention of Jesus' mind is wordlessly accomplished and the deformity is made right again.

According to the Pharisees' way of looking at the world, the man's hand was deformed because of the sin in his life. Jesus' ability to heal should be the clearest sign to them that he is the one who has come to "preserve life." But they are unable or unwilling to look beyond the breaking of one of their rules and see a miracle. The very ones who would so stubbornly argue about which way preserves life, leave the synagogue intent on killing Jesus.

PRAY: *Ask God to show you any ways in which you have elevated human rules over the life-giving rule of Christ.*

Simple, Not Easy

Then the Pharisees went out and began to
plot with the Herodians how they might kill Jesus.

MARK 3:6

I must ask myself, am I unable to see Jesus' miracles because they threaten my petty rules? Or could I possibly be the one with the deformity, waiting to hear his simple, authoritative command to stretch out my hand, my life, and see it transformed by his grace?

Following Jesus, the rule breaker, sometimes means going places and doing things the world forbids us to do. His command is always simple: "Get up and walk," "Follow me," "Stretch out your hand," "Take up your cross." Yet if we obey, we will inevitably find a formidable host arrayed against us. *Simple* does not necessarily mean *easy*.

APPLY: *What simple but not necessarily easy command is Christ giving you today?*

MONDAY *A Strained Homecoming*

After Jesus and his disciples arrived in Capernaum,
the collectors of the two-drachma tax came to Peter.

MATTHEW 17:24

Peter's familiar hometown, Capernaum, seemed to have changed as he and Jesus made their way back to Peter's house, their base of operations in Galilee. The disciples were still trying to cope with what Jesus had just revealed to them, that he was soon to die. Jesus' promise of resurrection might have provided a measure of comfort to Peter and the others, if only they had been able to grasp it.

Jesus returns to Capernaum to gather strength for the final confrontation in Jerusalem. Immediately some tax collectors confront Peter, inquiring as to whether or not his master pays the temple tax.

Sometimes in the Gospels the miracle is not the point of the story. Such is the case with the account of the coin in the fish's mouth.

JOURNAL: *Recall a time that you were exhausted and needed to gather strength for a coming ordeal. What demands came along to irritate and distract you? How did you respond?*

The Wrong Answer?

As servants of God, live as free people,
yet do not use your freedom as a pretext for evil.

1 PETER 2:16

The tax collectors who confronted Peter were not the same sort of tax collectors as Matthew, who represented the Romans. They were from the synagogue, and this tax was a Jewish one. It was a voluntary tax, which is why it was open to question. It was the commonly accepted custom of the day that religious teachers were exempt from this tax. The fact that the temple tax collectors came to ask at all is another indication that Jesus' reputation in Capernaum had begun to erode.

Peter automatically, as if conditioned by a lifetime of submitting to synagogue authority, answers, "Yes, he does." As soon as the words left his lips he felt that it was the wrong answer.

JOURNAL: *Peter apparently answered without thinking, something for which he was well known. What are some areas of your life where you respond without thinking, whether through habit, conditioning or some other cause? What steps can you take to become more aware of how you answer and to answer more thoughtfully?*

"From whom do the kings of the earth collect duty and taxes—
from their own sons or from others?"
"From others," Peter answered.
"Then the sons are exempt," Jesus said to him.

MATTHEW 17:25-26

I t is Jesus who speaks first when Peter comes in the door. "What do you think, Simon?" he says with tiredness in his voice that matches Peter's. Peter cannot remember Jesus ever asking him what he thought in this way. "Who pays taxes, sons or foreigners?" It seems a fair enough question.

"Why, foreigners of course," Peter replies.

"So the sons are exempt," Jesus says.

Given Jesus' words, we would expect his answer to mean "No, we won't pay the tax." Jesus is the Son, and he is not subject to any tax. But things have changed for him and his disciples in Capernaum. He is being treated in many ways like a foreigner.

APPLY: *As a Christian, in what circumstances do you feel that you are an out-sider? How do you deal with your feelings?*

THURSDAY

An Unrecorded Miracle

"But so that we may not offend them, go to the lake and throw out your line.
Take the first fish you catch; open its mouth and you will find a four-drachma coin.
Take it and give it to them for my tax and yours."

MATTHEW 17:27

Peter reaches behind the door and takes his line and hook from the peg where he always leaves them hanging. He goes down to the shoreline, puzzled that after being called to fish for people, he is being sent to fish for fish once more. And he wonders, *Since when does Jesus not want to offend these people? From the start he has gone out of his way to confront them.*

I find Jesus' statement about not wanting to offend anyone to be the most miraculous and mysterious part of the story. Incredibly, Matthew leaves out the fulfillment of the miracle. We can only assume that everything happened as Jesus said it would. But perhaps the miracle was not the point.

PRAY: *Pray that you will obey the Lord even when he asks for the unexpected. Trust his purposes for you and for others who are involved.*

FRIDAY

An Uninterrupted Evening

> *For it is God's will that by doing right*
> *you should silence the ignorance of the foolish.*

1 PETER 2:15 NRSV

Jesus' response and his provision of the unseen miracle is for the benefit of both himself and Peter. These two tired servants of God had stumbled back home to find, not a flock of the faithful, but demanding religious people waiting for them at the door.

Knowing that the least indiscretion would mean more conflict, Jesus chose to exercise his awesome power to make appear out of nowhere enough money to pay the fee. All this so that Jesus and Peter might share an uninterrupted evening together of talk and meal fellowship, since in a few days one of them would be leaving that place never to return.

PRAY: *Thank the Lord that he cares for your basic needs for rest, food, conversation and quiet.*

Choose Your Battles

Honor everyone. Love the family of believers.
Fear God. Honor the emperor.

1 PETER 2:17 NRSV

The commentaries often quote Matthew 22:21: "Give to Caesar what is Caesar's, and to God what is God's," as though that statement explains it all. But this was not Caesar's tax; it was, in effect, God's. And had not Peter already plainly confessed Jesus to be God's Son?

There seemed to be every reason for Jesus *not* to pay the tax and to deliberately cause offense. But mysteriously, he chose not to do so. He elected not to exercise his and Peter's rights as children of God.

Maybe Jesus simply needed the heat to be off for a few days to recover and prepare for the final trip to Jerusalem and his Passion. Perhaps he was only choosing his battles. Why get caught up in something so petty when infinitely larger struggles are about to present themselves?

APPLY: *Where are you in danger of being caught up in a petty struggle which will distract you from more important issues? How can you exempt yourself from the struggle?*

MONDAY *The Stumbling Block*

He will become a sanctuary, a stone one strikes against;
for both houses of Israel he will become a rock one stumbles over—
a trap and a snare for the inhabitants of Jerusalem.
And many among them shall stumble; they shall fall and be broken;
they shall be snared and taken.

ISAIAH 8:14-15 NRSV

A stumbling block. A scandal. Few of us ever think of Jesus in those terms, yet both the Old and New Testaments present him that way. The prophet Isaiah understood, perhaps better than any of the prophets, that when the Messiah would come, he would be an offense, a scandal. That is why he said, in another place, that the Messiah would be despised and rejected, a man of sorrows and familiar with suffering.

The scandal fanned into flame when the ministry of Jesus began. Now it seemed that everyone who came into contact with Jesus stumbled because of him.

JOURNAL: *How have you experienced Jesus as a stumbling block?*

Not Immune from Stumbling

But when John rebuked Herod the tetrarch because of Herodias, his brother's wife,
and all the other evil things he had done, Herod added this to them all:
He locked John up in prison.

LUKE 3:19-20

John the Baptist heard that Jesus had gone back to Galilee to preach and teach. We can only assume that John expected Jesus to come and get him out of prison, by whatever means. The Baptist believed himself deserted by his close friend and relative.

If anyone should have been immune from stumbling because of Jesus, it was John the Baptist. From the womb John knew who Jesus was, since his mother Elizabeth told Mary, "The instant I heard your voice, my baby leaped for joy!" (see Luke 1:44). The unborn John recognized even the unborn Jesus! It is John who first spoke of the dignity of Jesus and exclaimed, "Behold the Lamb of God!" The Baptist should have known better.

APPLY: *What would you say to someone who felt abandoned by Christ? If you feel that way now, what do you wish someone would say to you?*

A Startling Question

"Should we expect someone else?"

MATTHEW 11:3

In his despair, John sent some of his disciples to Jesus with a staggering question: "Are you the one who was to come, or should we expect someone else?" It is the most startling question in the New Testament. It reveals that even John the Baptist—who had leaped in his mother's womb, who had heard the voice of God, who had first proclaimed Jesus as the Lamb of God—has stumbled because of Jesus.

PRAY: *Pray that you will always take Christ as he is, and that you will never look for another.*

The Radical Kingdom

> *Jesus replied, "Go back and report to John what you hear and see:*
> *The blind receive sight, the lame walk, those who have leprosy are cured,*
> *the deaf hear, the dead are raised, and the good news is preached to the poor."*

MATTHEW 11:4-5

From his cell John was unable to see the precious glimpses of the radical, unorthodox kingdom that was entering history with the presence of Jesus. In his mind this kingdom was about the Messiah overcoming the Romans, fighting fire with fire. Never could he have dreamed of a kingdom where the King dies for the enemies he loves. Not in his wildest dreams could John, the dreamer, have imagined a kingdom where the fire of hate would be conquered by the living water of love.

Jesus' answer to John provides a glimpse of the new kingdom. The kingdom which Jesus ushered into the world is as unlikely and inconceivable as the servant shape of his life. So unorthodox is this kingdom that John himself almost misses it!

JOURNAL: *How is the new kingdom of Christ radically different from the world's idea of a kingdom?*

Mistaken Expectations

"And blessed is anyone who takes no offense at me."

MATTHEW 11:6 NRSV

The heart of our offense with Jesus is that he fails to meet our expectations. The priests and Pharisees expected a different sort of Messiah. It never occurred to John the Baptist that he would end up in prison. That, I believe, is the heart of the scandal. If it is truly Jesus himself you are getting close to, he will fail to meet your expectations sooner or later and you will stumble, like all the rest. Everyone who comes to know Jesus stumbles because of him.

APPLY: *What are some of your expectations of Jesus which he has not fulfilled? How have your ideas of him changed as a result? How have you changed as a result?*

Another Jesus?

> *I am astonished that you are so quickly deserting the one who called you*
> *by the grace of Christ and are turning to a different gospel—*
> *which is really no gospel at all.*

GALATIANS 1:6

Jesus always fails to meet our wrong expectations. He calls us to do impossible things or to become something we think we could never become. This is his way of teaching us how much we need him. He breaks us to pieces so that he can put us back together in his image.

Another Jesus is preached in America. He is different altogether. He never does anything unexpected. He is safe and predictable and easy to follow. He answers every prayer that is formulated correctly. He is easily stepped over. That is not the Jesus of the Bible.

APPLY: *Consider false ideas of Jesus which you have heard. Why do you think people find them attractive? Resolve to reject any false gospel and follow only the real Jesus of the Bible.*

MONDAY *Who Can Accept It?*

> Jesus said to them, "I tell you the truth, unless you eat the
> flesh of the Son of Man and drink his blood, you have no life in you.
> Whoever eats my flesh and drinks my blood has eternal life,
> and I will raise him up at the last day." . . .
> On hearing it, many of his disciples said,
> "This is a hard teaching. Who can accept it?"

JOHN 6:53-54, 60

Up until this point, Jesus' ministry had been primarily successful and well received. But Jesus understands that his misplaced popularity poses a significant threat to his real ministry. In the most offensive terms he can possibly come up with, he speaks the truth about what being the Passover Lamb of God means. The focus of the Passover is the eating of the Passover lamb. Jesus has simply and graphically put two and two together for them. This sets the scene for the scandal, failure and rejection that will follow. Jesus' own disciples will stumble because of him.

JOURNAL: *How could Jesus' popularity pose a threat to his real ministry—both during his lifetime and today?*

From this time many of his disciples turned back and no longer followed him.
"You do not want to leave too, do you?" Jesus asked the Twelve.

JOHN 6:66-67

In the face of his bloody, sickening and scandalous words, many of his disciples decided that enough was enough. They could bear the burden of the scandal no longer, and so many of them began to leave. The grammar of Jesus' query indicates that the question expects the answer "No."

The true test of discipleship is following Jesus not when the crowd is along for the ride but following him when no one else sees any sense in following him at all.

PRAY: *Perhaps you are faced with the decision of going against your family or friends in order to follow Christ. Or perhaps you know someone else who is faced with that choice. Pray for the Lord's help, strength and peace.*

WEDNESDAY

To Whom Shall We Go?

Simon Peter answered him, "Lord, to whom shall we go?
You have the words of eternal life."

JOHN 6:68

Simon's response to Jesus, spoken through slightly clenched teeth, represents an entirely different tone than his great confession "You are the Christ." In the context of scandal and rejection by the departing disciples, the tone here is one of loyal despair.

The dilemma: Jesus is indeed a scandalous Lord, but there is no place else to go! He is the Lord; he alone possesses infinitely more than the bread he has just doled out to the hungry and confused crowd. He is the Bread of Life, the true Manna that has come down from heaven. The words that fall from his lips are alive and life-giving, no matter what scandalous effect they may have.

PRAY: *Tell the Lord that he is your only hope, your Way, Truth and Life. Thank him for his gift of eternal life and for his life within you.*

"We believe and know that you are the Holy One of God."

JOHN 6:69

Peter and the others he speaks for will stay to the end only because there is no place else to go. If there were another option, they might have left like the others. It is only after this defining moment that Peter will begin to assert that he is willing to die with Jesus. He has begun to understand that all this may indeed end in death.

Each of us, if we follow Jesus closely, that is, biblically, will come to the same moment Peter came to in the sixth chapter of John.

JOURNAL: *What does it mean to say that Jesus is "the Holy One of God"? Write your thoughts about each of the five words, including "the" and "of."*

Shaking My Fist

Whoever has the Son has life;
whoever does not have the Son of God does not have life.

1 JOHN 5:12 NRSV

After a series of tragedies in my family, I went out in the field behind the place where I was living and literally shook my fist at God. "If this is the sort of thing you do, I don't want any part of you!" I screamed through my tears. In time I began to understand Jesus as the stumbling stone. I poured my understanding into a recording and then went about the country telling everyone the message I was still barely able to understand.

If you follow Jesus there will be a time when, like the disciples, you will see him in a new, unexpected way, in a light you never dreamed of or wanted to see him. He will fail to meet your expectations. You might lose a child. You might get cancer. After a lifetime of ministry you might feel rejected. You will experience him in a way that has caused countless of his other disciples to say, "This is hard; who can accept it?"

JOURNAL: *What is the most difficult test of faith you have ever experienced? Write how you feel about it, whether it is resolved now or not. Let your written words lead you to prayer, whether written, silent or out loud.*

Real Discipleship

Aware that his disciples were grumbling about this,
Jesus said to them, "Does this offend you?
What if you see the Son of Man ascend to where he was before!"

JOHN 6:61-62

Here is precisely the point where real discipleship begins. You and I have only two choices. We can leave with the others. After all, it really is too much, isn't it? Or we can realize what Peter understood as he clutched on to Jesus with the last fading shred of faith he could muster. He was right, you know. There is no other place to go, no other way.

You can choose, right now.

PRAY: *Bring your unanswered questions to the Lord. As you pray, consciously choose Jesus over every other idea or idol or attraction which appeals to you.*

Fall

MONDAY

Lord, What Were You Thinking?

> When the LORD began to speak through Hosea, the LORD said to him,
> "Go, take to yourself an adulterous wife and children of unfaithfulness,
> because the land is guilty of the vilest adultery in departing from the LORD."

HOSEA 1:2

If you are honest with God (and there's no use not being honest with him), when you read the opening passage of Hosea, you have to ask, "Lord, what were you thinking?" As if it were not difficult enough being a prophet, why place on Hosea's shoulders the intolerable burden of an unfaithful wife? It seems to make no sense.

You will notice that when God gave this bizarre command to Hosea, God did not use her name. This is probably because Hosea already knew exactly who God was talking about. Her name was Gomer. She was notorious for her unfaithfulness. Nonetheless, in obedience to the command, the prophet took her home to be his wife.

JOURNAL: *What do you think of God's strange command to Hosea? What good do you think could possibly come from Hosea's obedience?*

The Pain Is the Point

> *The LORD said to me, "Go, show your love to your wife again,*
> *though she is loved by another and is an adulteress.*
> *Love her as the LORD loves the Israelites,*
> *though they turn to other gods and love the sacred raisin cakes."*
> *So I bought her for fifteen shekels of silver and about a homer and a lethek of barley.*

HOSEA 3:1-2

You would hope that living with a person for whom one of the books of the Bible is named might have some impact on Gomer's behavior. It did. She got worse! Hosea alludes to the fact that she became a prostitute and that Hosea was forced to buy her back for fifteen shekels and a measure of barley.

It would be difficult to describe the emotional pain Hosea must have endured because of this impossible relationship. But the pain is the point. Through Hosea's suffering, God was doing something truly amazing: inviting the prophet into his own emotional life. Hosea and the Lord shared something in common: they were both married to unfaithful women, for in Scripture Israel is called the "wife" of the Lord.

APPLY: *Is the idea that God suffered new for you? When has obeying the Lord brought you pain?*

WEDNESDAY *An Enormous Price*

> *You are not your own; you were bought at a price.*
> *Therefore honor God with your body.*

1 CORINTHIANS 6:19-20

Two points should be made here. First, God uses everything, most especially suffering. Hosea was being called to participate in the sufferings of God and thereby to become acquainted with his heart. Hosea's pain uniquely prepared him to better represent the Lord.

Second, by buying Gomer back, Hosea demonstrated prophetically what God would someday do for us through Jesus. Like Gomer, we are habitually unfaithful, and yet we have been bought back at an enormous price.

PRAY: *Thank God for the enormous price he paid for you in the death of his Son.*

He Will Do the Cleaning

Come, let us return to the LORD.

HOSEA 6:1

The story of Hosea and Gomer is not a pretty story, not an elementary Sunday school type story that you would want to share with a roomful of children. Nevertheless it's a true story, even though there are scholars who say something so bizarre couldn't really have happened.

Did you notice that Hosea did not demand that Gomer clean up her act before he bought her back? Neither does God demand that we clean up our act before we come to him. He only bids us to come. He'll do the cleaning.

PRAY: *Confess any sin that the Lord brings to your conscience. Thank him for his cleansing which only he can accomplish.*

Likely to Stray

> *After two days he will revive us;*
> *on the third day he will restore us,*
> *that we may live in his presence.*

HOSEA 6:2

When we look at ourselves and invite God to look at us, we see that we are Gomer, the unfaithful bride. He called us into the intimacy of walking with him, and we have broken faith.

In sincere repentance we turn to Jesus. We come to him not on the basis of our good works or faith, but because he first loved, called and bought us back. We acknowledge the price he paid for us. And we ask him to keep a close watch on us, because if left to ourselves, we are likely to stray once more.

PRAY: *Ask the Lord to keep you faithful to him no matter what. Confess that left to yourself you will wander from him. Thank him for his constant faithfulness to you.*

The God Who Has Chosen Us

The LORD himself goes before you and will be with you;
he will never leave you nor forsake you.
Do not be afraid; do not be discouraged.

DEUTERONOMY 31:8

God is not necessarily the God we would have chosen, but neither could we have dreamed up nor imagined such a God: a God, the immediacy of whose presence is incarnate in us by his indwelling Spirit, a God who is committed to the throes of completing this labor of indwelling us, of being born in and through us. It is his deepest desire. It is the greatest of all his wordless miracles. And yet we are unsatisfied with him and want more. As Walter Brueggemann says, he is not the God any of us would have chosen, but he is the God who has chosen us.

JOURNAL: *Consider today's Scripture, Deuteronomy 31:8. How is it welcome news to you right now? What situations do you face in which you desperately need those words?*

M O N D A Y *Not Provision but Presence*

And surely I am with you always, to the very end of the age.

MATTHEW 28:20

Who is Jesus for you? How is faithfulness written on his face? Might he impossibly be the very image of the God whose disturbing faithfulness to us looks like incarnation? Could it be that he came not to wave the magic wand and make the cancer go away, but to enter into our sufferings? Could it possibly be true that the best show of faithfulness is not the healing or the unexpected check, but the unthinkable truth that God has chosen to be with us through it all? Could it be that the greatest miracle is not provision, but presence?

APPLY: *In what situations do you most need to know that God is with you? What are some practical ways you can you remind yourself of his presence?*

God's Deepest Desire

> *I will put my dwelling place among you, and I will not abhor you.*
> *I will walk among you and be your God, and you will be my people.*

We have answers in abundance, answers that seek to settle things once and for all, answers that often stop the imagination dead in its tracks. What we often lack are good questions, questions that drive us to new and deeper places of intimacy and understanding of who Jesus is and what he means. Sometimes a substantive question, even an unanswerable one, can accomplish more in us than a bookshelf of answers.

Here is a good question: *What is the deepest desire in the heart of God?*

You would expect the answer to such a significant question to echo through the Scriptures again and again. And if what we believe about Jesus of Nazareth is true, you should see that same answer written large across his perfect life.

JOURNAL: *How would you answer the question, "What is the deepest desire in the heart of God?" If you aren't sure, note several possible answers.*

> But the LORD God called to the man, "Where are you?"

GENESIS 3:9

God calls out to Adam, "Where are you?" He does not ask because he does not know where Adam is. God's question is an invitation to come take a walk, to share presence, in spite of Adam's disobedience. Though the first couple demonstrated their desire to disobey and walk away from God, still he called out, inviting them to come and be with him. The deepest desire of God's heart is to be *with us*.

Although he knows the answer, every moment God calls out to you and me that same ancient question: "Where are you?"

APPLY: *When have you wanted to hide from God? How did he encourage you to come out and face him? What happened as a result?*

He Came to Us

> *He came to that which was his own, but his own did not receive him.*
> *Yet to all who received him, to those who believed in his name,*
> *he gave the right to become children of God.*

JOHN 1:11-12

The incarnation of Jesus provides the final answer to our question *What is the deepest desire in the heart of God?* For what is the incarnation but the enfleshment of the deepest desire of God's heart, to be with us? After all, when you think of the person you love the most, isn't your deepest desire to be with that person?

On the cross, through the breaking of Jesus' heart, the fulfillment of the deepest desire of the Father's heart became a reality. *Immanuel* perfectly describes who Jesus is: *God with us!* What more could God have done to make it possible for him to be with us, and for us to be with him?

PRAY: *Thank the Lord that he is "God with us." Pray that you will want to be with him as much as he wants to be with you.*

No Longer Strangers

I was a stranger and you invited me in.

MATTHEW 25:35

Jesus Christ, the Messiah, the Son of God, came to this world a stranger. Jesus himself said, "I was a stranger and you invited me in." In effect he stated that not only had he come *as* a stranger, but he had come *for* the stranger.

Jesus was estranged not because he wasn't what he should have been but rather because the world wasn't what it should be. Even though the world had been created through him, it didn't recognize him.

If you invite the stranger in, Jesus says, it's as if you have invited him. He has come so no one has to be a stranger ever again, including you and me—at least not strangers to each other and to him.

APPLY: *Look for a stranger to invite in to your place of worship, and continue to look for strangers to welcome this coming week.*

SATURDAY/SUNDAY

To Lift the Veil

The reason the world does not know us is that it did not know him.

1 JOHN 3:1

After you've been a Christian for long enough, you discover a paradox: Once you become intimate with God you become even more a stranger to the world, for people in the world would have us groan all the more for knowing him. If the world did not recognize Jesus, then how much less can we expect it to recognize those who belong to him, unless he gives us the grace, from time to time, to lift the veil of his incarnation in us and show the world his wonderful work of re-creation.

JOURNAL: *Does it surprise you that the world did not—and does not—recognize the Son of God? Why do you answer as you do?*

M O N D A Y

The Shape of God's Faithfulness

> *In the land of Uz there lived a man whose name was Job.*
> *This man was blameless and upright;*
> *he feared God and shunned evil.*

JOB 1:1

The faithfulness of God is celebrated throughout the Bible. In fact when the word *faithfulness* appears in the Psalms, it is always God's faithfulness which is in view. Who wouldn't want to give their lives to such a God as this?

But then Job enters our uncluttered theological world, and the picture drastically changes. Job, the righteous one, who should be heir to all the promises of God and more, inherits instead unspeakable suffering. The leprous man seated in the ashes forces us to wrestle with the shape of God's faithfulness.

JOURNAL: *When have you questioned God's faithfulness? How was your faith affected by the experience?*

A Predictable God?

> Naked I came from my mother's womb,
> and naked I will depart.
> The LORD gave and the LORD has taken away;
> may the name of the LORD be praised.

JOB 1:21

Before we can start to look at Job, we must face up to a truth about ourselves. The "god" we think we need is faithful in ways we understand and expect, and he expresses faithfulness in the ways we choose. There is such a "god"; in fact there are many of them, constructed of small snippets of Bible verses glued together with human reason and need. This "god" always moves in predictable ways, according to the given formula. His faithfulness always feels good. It almost always ends in bankable results. But this is not the God of the Bible.

APPLY: *Do you tend to want God's faithfulness to end in obvious and predictable results? What are the dangers of such expectations?*

A Serious Journey

> *Why is light given to those in misery,*
> *and life to the bitter of soul?*

Are you able to admit the possibility that, like Job, you may have been serving only your notion of God? Can you imagine coming to the place where, with Job, you will confess, "My ears had heard of you but now my eyes have seen you" (Job 42:5)?

This is an invitation to a serious and arduous journey. Perhaps you do not feel the call as yet to follow this road. If so, that's all right. The journey should not be started out of a simple desire to do better. It must be taken up in response to the call of God on your life. If you sense your heart resonating with the words of Job, and if you see the circumstances of your own life directing you this way, I invite you to come along.

PRAY: *Bring to the Lord whatever is your most serious and troubling question, without demanding an answer. Simply bring it to him in honest prayer.*

The Accuser in the Throne Room

Then the LORD said to Satan, "Have you considered my servant Job?
There is no one on earth like him; he is blameless and upright,
a man who fears God and shuns evil."
"Does Job fear God for nothing?" Satan replied.
"Have you not put a hedge around him and his household and everything he has?"

JOB 1:8-10

One frustration of reading the book of Job is the realization that he was not privy to the throne room scene. Job apparently did not know about the exchange that occurred between God and Satan. Who knows what difference it would have made as he entered into the confusion of his innocent suffering?

Satan is there doing what his name implies, *accusing* Job of serving God only because there is something in it for him. "Take away the blessing," the accuser hisses, "and Job will fold like a house of cards." But the book of Job is not a test so that God can learn whether Job will be faithful or not. From the beginning God knew, and we can only suppose that's why he boasted of his servant as he did.

APPLY: *As you consider your biggest problem, acknowledge that there are many things about it which you do not know, and which only God knows. How does that affect your outlook on the problem?*

God's Clear Authority

The LORD said to Satan,
"Very well, then, everything he has is in your hands,
but on the man himself do not lay a finger."

JOB 1:12

For me what is most disturbing about the throne room scene is also what I find most comforting about it, and that is God's clear authority over Satan. He must receive permission from the Lord before he can do anything to Job. God clearly limits how far he can go. The first prohibition protected Job's health; the second saved his life.

But how could the Father, who cherishes his son Job so much, allow such an attack to be unleashed upon him? While God himself did not inflict the suffering, he permitted it. Perhaps it was better that Job didn't know what was going on behind the scenes in heaven. If he had, I'm certain he would have preferred that God not boast about him!

JOURNAL: *Write your thoughts about suffering, whether your own or that of someone you care about.*

Not Unique

> *No testing has overtaken you that is not common to everyone.*
> *God is faithful, and he will not let you be tested beyond your strength,*
> *but with the testing he will also provide the way out*
> *so that you may be able to endure it.*

1 CORINTHIANS 10:13 NRSV

I don't pretend to understand the mystery of suffering as it is presented in the book of Job, but several things seem clear to me from the throne room scene.

The first is God's sovereignty over suffering. In the end, if we believe him to be the *Abba* that Jesus revealed, I wouldn't want it any other way. It's not as if there were two equal forces, like yin and yang, battling for control of the universe. God is sovereign even over suffering.

Second, I don't believe Job's story is unique. The throne room scene is an ongoing one. That is why Paul can say that we will never be tested beyond our ability to bear. On our behalf the Father is still limiting what the devil can do according to our frailties.

PRAY: *Pray for yourself and others that you will live in the truth of 1 Corinthians 10:13. Thank the Lord for his strength in times of testing. Pray that you will see the "ways out" which he shows you and not ignore them.*

MONDAY *Unprecedented Worship*

> *Job got up and tore his robe and shaved his head.*
> *Then he fell to the ground in worship.*
>
> JOB 1:20

No one had ever heard of a wind blowing from four directions at once. It struck Job's firstborn son's house where the brothers and sisters had gathered for one of their frequent parties. Everyone was killed, crushed by the weight of the collapsed ceiling and walls.

Job had already lost all his possessions. He seemed to cope fairly well with the news when the surviving messengers came one after the other. But now the pain had exploded exponentially. As he entered the wilderness of that suffering, Job did something remarkable. So far no one in the Bible had done anything remotely like it. The book says that Job fell down and *worshiped*.

JOURNAL: *What do you think the content of Job's worship might have been?*

Worship in the Wilderness

> *Let my people go, so that they may*
> *celebrate a festival to me in the wilderness.*
>
> EXODUS 5:1 NRSV

All true worship begins in the wilderness. The word *worship* comes from the old English *worth-ship*. To worship God is to celebrate his worth. In the wilderness, the Israelites learned what God was worth when he provided for their needs with manna, quail and water from the rock.

As he entered the wilderness of his grief, Job recognized that only God was worthy to receive the offering of his pain and confusion. He knew he had nowhere else to go but to God.

APPLY: *What is God worth to you? How does your worship express his worth?*

Wrestling with God

> What I feared has come upon me;
> what I dreaded has happened to me.
> I have no peace, no quietness;
> I have no rest, but only turmoil.

JOB 3:25-26

When Job fell to the ground under the crushing weight of his sorrow, he wondered if he would ever see God again. The God he thought he knew had disappeared from his sight. Job went into the wilderness deaf, dumb and blind to God. It is out of this confusion that all his laments flow.

Despite the stark silence of God and the incessant theological chatter of his friends, Job never let go, never stopped straining to hear. In the darkness of his confusion he wrestled with the shadowy angel of his suffering, refusing to release his grip until God showed up. That wrestling, that stubborn refusal, is where true worship begins. It is the most profound offering to God that we can give. It is the supreme recognition of his worth.

JOURNAL: *In your own experience what has been the connection between worship and suffering? Have you ever wrestled with the Lord as an act of worship?*

A Question-Answering God?

When Job's three friends, Eliphaz the Temanite, Bildad the Shuhite and Zophar the Naamathite, heard about all the troubles that had come upon him, they set out from their homes and met together by agreement to go and sympathize with him and comfort him. When they saw him from a distance, they could hardly recognize him; they began to weep aloud, and they tore their robes and sprinkled dust on their heads. Then they sat on the ground with him for seven days and seven nights. No one said a word to him, because they saw how great his suffering was.

JOB 2:11-13

To Job's friends, God's faithfulness always looked like doing, answering, healing, ultimately providing. In return for their works-righteousness, God was obliged to respond faithfully. But Job (whom God himself declared righteous) suffered every sort of pain and loss. In return for his righteousness, Job received suffering. Where was God's faithfulness?

In Job's world, God expressed faithfulness by crushing the enemies of the faithful. In Job's world, God was a question-answering God. He was seen to be faithful in providing wisdom. But the God Job met at the end of his painful journey expressed his faithfulness in a way that no one could have ever imagined.

JOURNAL: *When has the Lord expressed his faithfulness to you in a way you did not expect and perhaps did not even welcome at the time? How has the experience broadened your concept of God and deepened your faith in him?*

Now Trouble Comes

> Think how you have instructed many,
> how you have strengthened feeble hands.
> Your words have supported those who stumbled;
> you have strengthened faltering knees.
> But now trouble comes to you, and you are discouraged;
> it strikes you, and you are dismayed.

JOB 4 : 3 - 5

After the arrival of his friends and their week of silence, the onslaught begins. Job incessantly seeks to cry out in lament to God. In addition to their insinuations that Job is suffering because of his sin, his friends try to shush Job's lamenting. They believe that such heated conversation with God is blasphemy. Would not God take vengeance on the arrogance of a person like Job who challenges him to his face?

Could it be that Satan, having seen that death and disease would not be enough to force Job to let go of God, sent Job's "friends" armed with an even more insidious weapon—despair?

APPLY: *When you try to help someone, do you tend to talk too much? Or do you avoid a friend in trouble because you don't know what to say? Notice that Job's friends helped him the most when they came to him but refrained from speaking.*

True Friends

If only I knew where to find him;
if only I could go to his dwelling!
I would state my case before him
and fill my mouth with arguments.

JOB 23:3-4

Job's friends were wrong about God. God himself will later say so (Job 42:7). But Job was wrong as well. He was wrong to let himself be distracted. He was wrong to give up talking *to* God and resort to only talking *about* God.

Job calls out to those of us who are in the wilderness, "Beware!" It could be that your undoing will not be caused by death or disease, by cancer or the failed marriage. Your worst enemies could very well be disguised as friends. How do you know the difference? True friends will be willing to sit with you in silence, not for a week, but for as long as it takes. Your real friends will encourage you to keep talking to, crying out to, arguing with God.

PRAY: *Pray that you will know when to keep silent in the face of a friend's suffering. Thank the Lord for friends who have shown such wisdom to you.*

MONDAY

When the Equation Stops Working

Why does the Almighty not set times for judgment?
Why must those who know him look in vain for such days?

JOB 24:1

Job's life had been lived by a simple equation: be good and get blessed, be bad and receive punishment. The equation had always worked perfectly . . . until now. Had suffering not entered his life, Job would have happily remained in the comfortable life that "worked." Had he remained there, however, he would have never seen God.

Job's suffering confronts the equation and the seemingly predictable God behind it. His suffering presents a frightening mystery to his friends, who struggle to hold on to the equation as vehemently as Job tries to hold on to God.

APPLY: *Is there someone whose suffering presents a frightening mystery to you right now? Summon the courage to admit to God your confusion and even your anger.*

A Stunning New Understanding

Shall we accept good from God, and not trouble?

JOB 2:10

As we continue our journey on this difficult road with Job, we discover that God simply refuses to act in simple, easily understandable ways that coincide with our definition of what his faithfulness should look like. We plead, and yet the cancer rate among Christians remains the same as for those outside our faith. We beg for financial help, but when the looked-for check does not appear, we think we must not have had enough faith.

Those are the kinds of difficult questions that troubled Job. Either God was not being faithful to his promises (unthinkable!) or else Job didn't understand all that God's faithfulness meant. Job is poised on the edge of a stunning new understanding of God.

PRAY: *Thank God that he is bigger than our preconceived ideas about him. Thank him for new understanding.*

> *I know that my Redeemer lives*
> *and that in the end he will stand upon the earth.*

JOB 19:25

As he wrestles with the God he thought he knew, Job makes three stunning new realizations about the Lord. They fill in the gaps his suffering had exposed in the old equation.

First he sees the need for "someone" who can arbitrate between himself and God (9:33). Until now, Job thought he only needed his own righteousness.

Then Job reaches out to an unseen person he calls his "advocate" and "intercessor" (16:19-20). Without even knowing about the throne room scene, he senses that someone needs to intercede on his behalf before the throne of God.

Finally, Job cries out to his "Redeemer" (19:25). Before his suffering, he only felt the urge to do better or try harder. Now, having lost everything a person can lose, Job sees he doesn't simply need God's help; he needs to be redeemed.

JOURNAL: *Consider Jesus Christ the arbitrator, the advocate, the intercessor and the redeemer. How do you think Job came to such a remarkable understanding of the coming Messiah? What was the role of suffering in Job's understanding?*

From Law to Grace

> *The sacrifices of God are a broken spirit;*
> *a broken and contrite heart,*
> *O God, you will not despise.*

PSALM 51:17

The realizations Job makes throughout his book, David also makes in Psalm 51. He realizes that it is God who must create a clean heart in him; otherwise there will only be more adulteries with more Bathshebas. He understands that the blood of bulls and goats will never be sufficient. Like Job, David realizes that all he has left is all God wanted in the first place: a broken spirit and a contrite heart.

The journey is from works-righteousness to the righteousness that comes only from God, from law to grace, from Psalm 1 to Psalm 150, from obedience to praise.

PRAY: *Ask the Lord to cleanse you from any trace of works-righteousness. Offer him a broken spirit and a contrite heart.*

From Immaturity to Intimacy

I know that you can do all things;
no plan of yours can be thwarted.
You asked, "Who is this that obscures my counsel without knowledge?"
Surely I spoke of things I did not understand,
things too wonderful for me to know.

J O B   4 2 : 2 - 3

The Bible invites us on a journey from law to grace, from immaturity to an intimate relationship with the Father. Could this journey also be understood as simply a journey to God? From the simple beginnings of a Father who lovingly gives rules, to the intimacy of a relationship we can scarcely imagine?

Do you think Job could have ever arrived at his remarkable understanding of Jesus the Redeemer, without the pain that God allowed in his life? And do you recognize the need for understanding your own life as that same pilgrimage from immaturity to intimacy?

JOURNAL: *How would you describe your faith at its immature stage? How have you moved toward intimacy with God?*

The One Who Descends

He who descended is the very one who ascended higher than all the heavens,
in order to fill the whole universe.

EPHESIANS 4:10

Who is God for you? What does his faithfulness look like? Is he the predictable theological Entity, frozen on the throne? Or could he possibly, unimaginably be the God we meet in Job, the God we see in Jesus, who descends from the throne room where he has been dealing with the accusations of Satan, who shows up, having been moved there by Job's tears and ours?

Jesus comes into our lives unexpectedly, like a thief in the night. He meets us in the dark hallways of lost hope and suffering. He takes off the thief's mask, and behold, the face of compassion, eyes wet with our tears.

PRAY: *Jesus descended from the throne room to walk on earth and even to die for us. Praise him for coming to you and for you.*

MONDAY *Images of Hell*

> If I go to the east, he is not there;
> if I go to the west, I do not find him.

JOB 23:8

There are many images of hell. The Bible presents us with images of stinking sulfur, torturous flames and teeth-grinding pain. Popular culture has expanded upon these biblical images, Disney-fying them with devils with horns and pitchforks.

The lament literature of the Bible presents a more focused image of hell and perhaps even a more terrifying one. Hell happens in the laments when God looks away. Hell is when the light of his face disappears, when he seems to forget us, when he apparently falls asleep. That is where Job found himself.

JOURNAL: *What do you think of the idea that hell is the absence of God?*

The Hidden Face of God

How many wrongs and sins have I committed?
Show me my offense and my sin.
Why do you hide your face
and consider me your enemy?

JOB 13:23-24

"Why?" Job asks. "How long?" Job's pain keeps telling him that he needs answers from God, and God remains silent. If it can be imagined, Job's suffering from the perceived absence of God is greater than the pain of his many losses. He believes that the Lord gives and the Lord takes away (1:21). But what if what the Lord has taken away is himself? Job finds this idea unbearable. For Job, hell is the hidden face of God.

When God looks away, or even when we mistakenly think he has looked away, the experience of the absence of that Presence which is Light and Life is one of the closest experiences of hell we can ever know this side of eternity.

PRAY: *Talk to God even if you feel that he is absent. If you have the certainty of his presence but know someone who feels God is absent, pray for that person. Ask God to hold that person safe until he shows his face again.*

Out of the Storm

Then the LORD answered Job out of the storm.

JOB 38:1

J ob's lament-derived definition of hell brings into sharp focus the climax of the book, the moment when God finally reappears! In a sense God's appearing lifts Job out of his dark, lonely hell.

It has troubled theologians for centuries that when God appears, he offers no answers to the problem of Job's suffering, that in fact he asks a long string of infinitely harder questions. They fail to recognize the awesome fact that God's appearing is the answer. He has moved off the throne and become fully present for his suffering servant, Job.

JOURNAL: *Imagine that you are Job. You have complained out loud for many hours while God is silent. You think you will never hear God's voice again. And then, with no warning except a windstorm, he speaks to you. What do you expect to be the main subject of his words? What do you expect him to say about that subject? When God speaks only of his own greatness and the limited state of your knowledge, how do you respond?*

> *My ears had heard of you*
> *but now my eyes have seen you.*

JOB 42:5

God did not answer Job's questions or crush Job's enemies. He simply moved from the throne of chapter one and became present. His appearance is the only answer the book provides to the mystery of suffering.

The God of Job shows his faithfulness by showing up. He is the One whose faithfulness is more a matter of presence than provision. "I had heard about you," stammers Job, "but now my eyes see you." Job does not seem troubled that his questions are left unanswered. He doesn't seem to care that, for now, he has not gotten his possessions back. He has gotten God back! That is all that matters.

PRAY: *Praise the Lord that he is a God who is moved by our tears, who left the throne of our theological equations and actually entered into our situation!*

A Tear in the Eye of Faithfulness

> *"Where have you laid him?" [Jesus] asked.*
> *"Come and see, Lord," they replied.*
> *Jesus wept.*
>
> JOHN 11:34-35

The Lord Jesus is the God who shows up, who leaves the throne and becomes a man, who is moved by our tears, even to the point of weeping with and for us.

After hearing of the illness of his close friend Lazarus, Jesus appears to loiter for two frustrating days. As a result, Lazarus dies. Lazarus's sisters Martha and Mary appear with the same disappointed accusation on their lips: if only he had been there, their brother would not have died. If only you had fixed things, healed him, answered our prayers the way we wanted them answered. But, like his Father, Jesus had come to show that God is faithful to us in ways we could never have dreamed.

Jesus showed up and entered fully and painfully into the suffering of his friends. What Jesus changed forever was the image of the face of faithfulness. Not menacing, not judgmental; not with anger in its eyes but rather a tear.

PRAY: *Thank the Lord for his tears.*

Keep Moving Ahead

The LORD blessed the latter part of Job's life more than the first.

JOB 42:12

By his power and might, Jesus will destroy in us those false images of the God who exists only to bless and provide. You will discover that as you try to move into this understanding of the primacy of the presence of God over the provision of God, you will be tempted to move back, to lose the ground you've been given. Determine that, by grace, you will continue to move ahead on this difficult and dangerous road, always keeping the Word before you as a light.

APPLY: *Have you ever experienced a greater desire for the Lord's presence than for his provision? How would such an outlook change your life?*

M O N D A Y *A Spy's Report*

> *We wait for the blessed hope—*
> *the glorious appearing of our great God and Savior, Jesus Christ.*

TITUS 2:13

The Roman emperor Trajan had been waiting for a report about the troublesome sect called Christians. He had enlisted a spy named Pliny the Younger. When the report finally came, the emperor was disappointed by its brevity and lack of accusations: "They worship one Christ, whom they revere as God." Pliny's brief report also claimed that the Christians "gather early in the morning and sing a hymn" to this Christ whom they worship.

Earlier Roman reports had confused the name *Christos*, or Christ, for *Chrestus*, which was a common personal name given to a slave. It was an understandable mistake, considering the reputation of the Galilean carpenter who acted more like a slave than an anointed king.

JOURNAL: *Why is the idea of Christ as a slave rather than a king so startling? How does thinking of Jesus as Servant-Savior affect your worship?*

The Morning Hymn

> *Your attitude should be the same as that of Christ Jesus:*
> *Who, being in very nature God,*
> *did not consider equality with God something to be grasped,*
> *but made himself nothing,*
> *taking the very nature of a servant,*
> *being made in human likeness.*

PHILIPPIANS 2:5-7

Many scholars believe that the morning hymn which the early Christians sang is found in Philippians 2:6-11, which has come to be known as the *Carmen Christi, or* "Hymn to Christ." I find it touching that before this passage was ever made the topic of a theological debate, it was sung. Without reasoning and argumentation the early believers embraced these complex incarnational truths by means of a simple melody. "When the soul hears music it lets down its best guard," Socrates said. And so with music those early saints sang their way to a belief in the unbelievable. With their hearts as well as their minds, they embraced the mystery of the incarnation of Jesus.

PRAY: *Thank the Lord for becoming incarnate and walking on earth as a human being. Sing to him whatever song expresses for you the wonder of his incarnation.*

Humility and Servanthood

And being found in appearance as a man,
he humbled himself
and became obedient to death—
even death on a cross!

PHILIPPIANS 2:8

In the "Hymn to Christ" we see two concepts central to the life of Jesus: humility and servanthood. Jesus "made himself nothing" and "humbled himself," the early Christians sang. He took the form of a servant, though he might have grasped equality with God. This was the puzzling nature of the appearance of "God with us." In humility and as a servant, he came to live and die for us. God held up Jesus to us and said, "This is what it means to be created in my image!"

The obedience of Jesus was not obedience as an abstract concept, but vividly and radically portrayed in flesh and blood. It was obedience to death, even death on a cross!

APPLY: *What is most difficult for you about humility and servanthood? How does the example of Christ help you?*

The Song Takes Off!

> Therefore God exalted him to the highest place
> and gave him the name that is above every name,
> that at the name of Jesus every knee should bow,
> in heaven and on earth and under the earth,
> and every tongue confess that Jesus Christ is Lord,
> to the glory of God the Father.
>
> PHILIPPIANS 2:9-11

The chorus of this early hymn must have resolved from a minor to a major key. I hear sopranos screeching and baritones giving it everything they've got. In the back someone breaks out the tambourine. The song takes off!

In the chorus the concepts of the verse are transformed from humility to exaltation and from servanthood to lordship. The chorus opens with "therefore," which points to the connection between the two pairs of concepts. Observe the radical reversal from the One who refused glory and made himself nothing to the One who is exalted to the highest place! Remember the One who took upon himself the form of a servant? Now every tongue confesses that same person as Lord. Every knee is bowed before him as well. Jesus Christ is Lord!

JOURNAL: *As much as possible, imagine the scene of every knee bowing to Jesus and every tongue confessing that he is Lord. What do you see? What do you hear?*

More Than a Picture

And we, who with unveiled faces all reflect the Lord's glory,
are being transformed into his likeness with ever-increasing glory,
which comes from the Lord, who is the Spirit.

2 CORINTHIANS 3:18

The ancient song which is now part of Philippians paints a wonderful picture of the incarnation of Christ and of a powerful process that is at work in the world. With one dark verse and one brilliant chorus, we see Jesus and ourselves in a new light. The apostle Paul was giving the Philippian Christians more than a picture of Christ. He was suggesting servanthood and radical obedience as a pattern for their lives—and for ours.

As we sing to the glory of Christ we are changed into his image. We are humble servants who through our obedience will someday be glorified and exalted.

APPLY: *How have you seen the Lord transform your character? Where do you still need transformation? How will you continue to focus on him and so be transformed?*

> *For all who exalt themselves will be humbled,*
> *and those who humble themselves will be exalted.*

LUKE 14:11 NRSV

Jesus' life demonstrated what it means for us to be created in God's image (or rather re-created, since re-creating is what we need). He tells us that whoever desires to be great must first become a servant. That process, which was so powerfully seen in the life of Jesus, is at work in our own lives as well. The way is humility, servanthood and radical obedience. It is something which people like the Emperor Trajan and Pliny the Younger and so many in our own day can never understand.

JOURNAL: *How do you react to Luke 14:11? Do Jesus' words strike you as hopeful? threatening? frightening? challenging? something else?*

MONDAY

One of Us

> *Since the children have flesh and blood,*
> *he too shared in their humanity so that by his death he might destroy*
> *him who holds the power of death—that is, the devil—*
> *and free those who all their lives were held in slavery by their fear of death.*

HEBREWS 2:14-15

We focus so much on the fact that Jesus died for us, we sometimes forget that he also lived for us and lives for us still. If Jesus had simply come as himself, and not as one of us, the Bible makes it quite clear that we could not have borne the sight of his presence, any more than Moses could have looked directly at the face of God.

Imagine what it would be like to be at the Father's side one moment and struggling to sleep in a cattle trough the next. Imagine what it would be like to go from hearing the praise of angels to suffering the taunts of stupid people. The cost to Jesus is an indication of the incredible value of what he came to give us. And because no one will ever fully know what that cost Jesus, we can only begin to understand the incredible value of his gift to us.

PRAY: *Thank God for his incredible gift of Jesus. Ask him to show you some special way you can honor him today.*

God with Us

> *All this took place to fulfill what the Lord had said through the prophet:*
> *"The virgin will be with child and will give birth to a son,*
> *and they will call him Immanuel"—which means, "God with us."*

MATTHEW 1:22-23

Susan and I got married in December. The church was already decorated for Christmas, and so we congratulated ourselves on saving money. In my nervousness I forgot much of what was said and done around us. When I see a picture of us together on that day, I honestly can't remember how I felt.

I do clearly remember the homily, however. With the promise of Christmas so close and our new life together just about to begin, our pastor, Dr. Bill Lane, spoke a word of great power and promise. The word was *Immanuel:* "God with us." No better name could have been spoken to Susan and me. *Immanuel.* It is a wonderful word for anyone to hear, married or not, in this or any other time. For it means Jesus is with us every moment of every hour of every day of our lives.

JOURNAL: *What do you think of when you hear or read the phrase "Immanuel—God with us"? What difference does it make that God is with us?*

The Word Became Flesh

The Word became flesh and made his dwelling among us.

JOHN 1:14

The implications of the name *Immanuel* are both comforting and unsettling. Comforting, because he has come to share the danger and the drudgery of our everyday lives. He desires to weep with us and to wipe away our tears. What seems most bizarre, Jesus Christ, the Son of God, longs to share in and to be the source of the laughter and the joy we all too rarely know.

It is one thing to claim that God looks down upon us from a safe distance and speaks to us (via long distance, we hope). But to say that he is right here is to put ourselves and him in a totally new situation. He is no longer the calm and benevolent observer in the sky, the kindly old caricature with the beard. His image becomes that of Jesus, who wept and laughed, who fasted and feasted, and who, above all, was fully present to those he loved. He was there with them. He is here with us.

APPLY: *When are you most aware that God is with you? When would you rather he regarded you from a distance? How can you more fully acknowledge him in your sorrows and in your joys?*

When they call to me, I will answer them;
I will be with them in trouble,
I will rescue them and honor them.

PSALM 91:15 NRSV

Time and time again, both in sorrow and in joy, Susan and I have become aware of Jesus' presence. As we looked into each new baby's face, bits and pieces of which reminded us of ourselves and our families, we knew the joyful sense of sharing that moment with him. At a totally different time, in the middle of an argument, we've experienced his disturbing presence, which convicted us of failing to be to each other all he would want us to be.

Most incredible, however, are the times we know he is with us in the midst of our daily, routine lives. In the middle of cleaning the house or driving somewhere in the pickup, he stops us both in our tracks and makes his presence known. Often it's in the middle of the most mundane task that he lets us know he is there with us. We realize, then, that there can be no "ordinary" moments for people who live their lives with Jesus.

JOURNAL: *When has Jesus surprised you with his presence? How does his presence lift any moment out of the ordinary?*

Jesus the Reconciler

See, the home of God is among mortals.
He will dwell with them; they will be his peoples,
and God himself will be with them.

REVELATION 21:3 NRSV

In the garden, Adam and Eve experienced separation, not only from God and the garden, but also from each other. The bitterness of their separation is felt in one way or another in every human relationship you and I will ever know. It is also experienced between the nations.

At his first coming, Jesus began dismantling all the chaos of separation. He demonstrated that it was possible for individuals, once separated by sin, to come together through forgiveness. We see the power of this demonstrated in the diversity of his disciples. Educated and uneducated, simple Jews and radical nationalists, loyalists and traitors, they were made one and presented as the firstfruits of the undoing.

But of course the central wound of the Fall is the separation between humanity and God himself. The coming of Jesus began to undo the great separation between ourselves and God.

APPLY: *Jesus reconciles us to each other and to God. How can you be a reconciler today?*

Knowing the Mystery

And I pray that you, being rooted and established in love,
may have power, together with all the saints, to grasp how wide and long and high and deep
is the love of Christ, and to know this love that surpasses knowledge.

EPHESIANS 3:17-19

A simple man, a carpenter from obscure Galilee, was not merely the representative of, but was God incarnate and man deified, "very God of very God," as the creed says. The Infinite contained in the ridiculously finite. Is *anyone* willing to raise a hand and say, "I understand"?

So what is our condition? Are we irrationalists, left to stumble about in the dark? No; the purpose of the mystery of Christ is not to blind our eyes but to open them to belief in him. The purpose is not to separate us into the "spiritual" and the "worldly," but to make us one as we try to live the mystery.

We are not irrationalists; we are believers. Only by believing do we "know." We do not claim to fully understand the mystery. It is because of the mystery, and not in spite of it, that we know. The mystery calls forth faith, giving us the ability to "know" with the heart as well as the mind.

APPLY: *Do you tend to know with your heart or with your mind? Knowing Christ involves both. Ask him to show himself in both your mind and your heart.*

M O N D A Y *Promises Are Costly*

I will put enmity
between you and the woman,
and between your offspring and hers;
he will crush your head,
and you will strike his heel.

GENESIS 3:15

Our God is the great maker of promises. His Word, the Bible, is quite simply a collection of the promises he has made to us. In the beginning God told Adam and Eve, I will send someone who will crush the head of the serpent. A promise. Most of the other promises in the Bible are only a variation on that theme. They concern Jesus, who would come to be known as the Promised One. Through all these promises, God was trying to give something of himself to Adam and to Israel and finally to us. The Bible tells us that when the Promised One finally came, the Lord poured all of himself into him.

In the fullness of time what God had desired to do through the ages happened: he gave all of himself to us through Jesus Christ, the Word of God, spoken at an incalculable price.

PRAY: *Thank God that he keeps his promises. Thank him especially for the Promised One, Jesus Christ. Pray that you will keep your promises to others and to him.*

A Promise Kept

> *She will give birth to a son, and you are to give him the name Jesus,*
> *because he will save his people from their sins.*

MATTHEW 1:21

Christmas is the celebration of the keeping of a promise.

Faith, in the Old Testament, is defined by a person's willingness to wait for the promises of God to come. Faith, in the New Testament, means following the Promised One.

In that Promised One, God gave to us all that he could give. Overwhelmed by his own desire to give, God sent the most treasured Gift to keep the promise he himself made. God chose to suffer the punishment which should have been inflicted on those who are guilty of breaking a promise. For those who see Christianity merely as a relationship in which we can ask God for things, Christmas reminds us that he has already given his all, his own Son.

Christianity is founded on a promise. Faith involves waiting on a promise. Our hope is based on a promise. God promised he would be "with us," not as an unseen ethereal force, but in the form of a person with a name: *Jesus.*

JOURNAL: *How do you respond to the statement "Christmas is the celebration of the keeping of a promise"?*

A Paradox and a Mystery

The angel said to her, "Do not be afraid, Mary, you have found favor with God.
You will be with child and give birth to a son, and you are to give him the name Jesus.
He will be great and will be called the Son of the Most High."

LUKE 1:30-32

Christmas is a struggle for my wife and me. Our ongoing war with the world seems to intensify as the decorations go up all over town. There is Christ's name, in every window. Sometimes there is even a statue of his sweet infant body, lying in some straw with shepherds and wise men standing around with blank porcelain expressions. Their faces convey the attitude of the world toward Christmas: blank, dazed and bewildered.

If people today would look at the birth of Jesus straight on, they would be puzzled that we should celebrate the birth of a baby who was born to die. The contradictions should be more than the world can take. If only Christianity could be seen for what it is—a paradox and a mystery. The beginning in that dirty stable is one of the greatest mysteries: the plainness and the greatness of Jesus, the grime and the glory. Wise men with gold in their hands and shepherds with sheep dung on their shoes. A smelly stable below and a shining star above. The birth of a gentle Lamb who was the fiercest Lion.

JOURNAL: *What is your greatest joy connected with Christmas? What is your greatest struggle?*

"How Can I Be Sure?"

Zechariah asked the angel, "How can I be sure of this?
I am an old man and my wife is well along in years."

LUKE 1 : 18

A quirk of human nature that attracted Luke's attention was the tendency of religious people to miss the deepest realities of Jesus' life, while simpler people grasped the heart of what Jesus was all about and responded in faith.

Zechariah was the elderly priest who would become the father of John the Baptist. We first meet him in the holy place of the temple. Only a curtain separates him from the Holy of Holies. Having drawn one of four lots, he stands in front of the altar, burning incense. Since there were approximately 20,000 priests in Israel, this would likely be his only chance to serve in the temple.

The angel Gabriel appears beside the altar of incense and announces to the old man that his prayers will be answered. He and his wife Elizabeth will have a son. And Zechariah can't believe it. A priest, in the holy place of the temple, receives a message from an angel with an answer to his own prayers and yet . . . responds in disbelief!

PRAY: *If Zechariah could respond in disbelief, so can any of us. Pray that you will be ready to receive the answers to your prayers.*

"I Am the Lord's Servant"

"I am the Lord's servant," Mary answered.
"May it be to me as you have said."

LUKE 1:38

In contrast to Zechariah, Luke draws a picture of a very different person. She is not in the temple, but a simple house. Though she is a descendant of David, she seems to serve no special purpose. She has no title. She is engaged to an obscure craftsman. Her name is Mary.

The angel Gabriel, who had appeared to Zechariah, also appears to Mary. The message Mary receives from the angel asks far more of her than the message he gave to Zechariah. And yet, how does she respond?

"I am the Lord's slave," she says.

For those of us who should know better, but fail, there is grace. The Lord eventually gave Zechariah a new song to sing (Luke 1:68-79). For those of us from whom the world expects nothing, God is ready to speak his Word and do his work and bless us in unimaginable ways.

APPLY: *What difficult task is the Lord calling you to take on? How are you responding? Can you pray your own variation of Mary's words in Luke 1:38?*

His mercy extends to those who fear him,
from generation to generation.

LUKE 1:50

A distinction of Luke's Gospel is his preoccupation with song. Only Luke recorded the songs of the angels, Mary, Zechariah and Simeon. As the birth of Jesus approached, new songs were born in the hearts of God's people. Luke was fascinated by it all. If we listen closely to the songs of the nativity, one theme echoes again and again: the mercy of God.

In the Old Testament, God defined himself by the term *hesed*. This is an untranslatable Hebrew word which is sometimes rendered *mercy, lovingkindness, covenant-faithfulness* or even *love*. It takes a whole sentence to even begin to translate the term, but this is a good place to start. When someone from whom I have a right to expect nothing, gives me everything, I experience *hesed*.

JOURNAL: *How have you experienced God's* hesed, *his lavish and undeserved mercy?*

MONDAY

All You Could Ever Want

> *For to us a child is born,*
> *to us a son is given,*
> *and the government will be on his shoulders.*
> *And he will be called*
> *Wonderful Counselor, Mighty God,*
> *Everlasting Father, Prince of Peace.*
>
> ISAIAH 9:6

All we could ever imagine, could ever hope for, Jesus is. He is the wise royal Counselor who fills us with wonder, who holds the tangled story lines of history and will one day bring true understanding between all individuals and nations. He is the God of Might, whose power can accomplish any and every task his holiness demands. His power we need not fear for he is also the Father Eternal who is tenderness itself and who is ever motivated by his everlasting love for his children. Finally, he is the Prince of Peace whose first coming has already transformed society but whose second coming will forever establish justice and righteousness. All this, and infinitely more, alive in an impoverished baby in a barn.

That is what Christmas means—to find in a place where you would least expect to find anything you want, everything you could ever want.

PRAY: *Honor Jesus Christ as the one who is everything you could ever want. Trust his all-sufficiency for all you need.*

He has been mindful
of the humble estate of his servant.
From now on all generations will call me blessed,
for the Mighty One has done great things for me—
holy is his name.

LUKE 1:48-49

*H*esed is what Mary means when she sings about her humble estate. She knows she has no right to expect anything on the basis of her own merits. Nevertheless, from now on all generations will call her blessed.

Hesed is also what Zechariah means when later he sings of the forgiveness of the people's sins because of "the tender mercy of our God" (Luke 1:78). And though he may not use the precise term, mercy is what Simeon is really singing about as he holds the little kicking baby in the courtyard of the temple. "A light for revelation to the Gentiles and for glory to your people Israel," he sings (Luke 2:32). What else but God's unspeakable *hesed* could make something like that happen?

APPLY: *What songs help you to especially appreciate God's mercy? Sing them to him today.*

A Baby and a Barn

She gave birth to her firstborn, a son.
She wrapped him in cloths and placed him in a manger,
because there was no room for them in the inn.

LUKE 2:7

It is our family Christmas tradition to pile in the car and go to a real working barn, with horses in their stalls and a barn cat on the prowl among the hay bales. There, together, we read the Christmas story by candlelight. The odor and the dark seem to press in against the fragile light of our candle.

The shabbiness of this setting reminds us of that other shabby place Jesus chooses every day to be born: the human heart, a place more filthy and cold than any stable. All this comes so much closer to reality for us than the singing Christmas trees or the huge services. They may have their place and might become a genuine part of the real celebration, but not without the smell of the straw and the bewildered animals who seem almost about to speak. A baby and a barn. Only with these things can the celebration be truly complete.

JOURNAL: *Are you able to keep in touch with the simplicity of Christ's birth, or do the trappings of Christmas distract you? What does the shabbiness of his birth tell you about God?*

T H U R S D A Y

The Stable and the Cross

This child is destined to cause the falling and rising of many in Israel,
and to be a sign that will be spoken against,
so that the thoughts of many hearts will be revealed.

LUKE 2:34-35

As our family gathers around our faint, flickering candle to read the Christmas story, the loneliness of the stable reminds us of the loneliness of another place on a hill outside Jerusalem. The rough trough seems almost as cruel a place as a cross. The infant cries we hear coming from the stable seem no less desperate than his final cry, and no less forsaken.

Celebrate? you say. Yes, most heartily, amidst the dung of the stable, which is, of course, the refuse of the world. Celebrate at the foot of that ghastly cross because it is the hope of the world. Gather around a cattle trough and celebrate a baby born in poverty and rejected, because he is the Savior of the world!

JOURNAL: *In what ways is it fitting to think of the cross at the same time we think of Jesus' birth? Why are both causes for celebration?*

Two Kinds of People

> The child's father and mother
> marveled at what was said about him.
>
> LUKE 2:33

Throughout his life, Jesus will preach, teach and demonstrate the mercy, the *hesed,* of God. He will tell parables about it and will redefine our relationship to the Father in the light of it. This unutterable mercy will cause many to lovingly forsake everything and follow him. Others will hate and reject the God they never knew precisely because they cannot possibly imagine such unimaginable mercy.

In his considerable wake Jesus will leave only two kinds of people: those who recognize that they are utterly undeserving and need mercy and those who refuse to see both their need and their inability to do anything to earn it. His teaching and preaching, his life, and most especially his death were a three-decades-long explanation of the mercy of God.

PRAY: *Pray for both kinds of people—those who recognize that they need God's mercy and those who still deny it. Thank God for showing his mercy to you.*

The Frailty of His Son

God chose the foolish things of the world to shame the wise;
God chose the weak things of the world to shame the strong.

1 CORINTHIANS 1:27

Though God is revealed as the loving Creator and Father in the Old Testament, by and large his power and might are the focus. Yet when Jesus the Son of God appears, power is not the focus, even though he does display his power at times. Jesus' ministry is characterized by weakness. The disciples are hardly a dazzling bunch of movers and shakers. In the end Jesus is rejected and crucified in weakness. How could El Shaddai, God Almighty, be the Father of such a Son? Jesus strikes no one dead for confronting him. He becomes tired and hungry. The ultimate paradox is that he dies.

Though God had spoken the universe into existence and displayed his power to the children of Israel, the most awesome accomplishment of El Shaddai was made possible only through the frailty of his only Son. Jesus died for you and me. By God's power he rose again, but we must never forget that first he died.

PRAY: *Ask God to use your weaknesses for his purposes.*

M O N D A Y

The Carpenter's Son

> "Where did this man get this wisdom and these miraculous powers?" they asked.
> "Isn't this the carpenter's son?"

MATTHEW 13:54-55

A simple carpenter stands in the shadow of the stable, in the shadow of history. People come and go. The shepherds have seen angels. The Magi have seen a star. Others have heard fantastic rumors. Some of them have come hundreds of miles. Some have only come across the street. The silent figure stands there watching them come and go, the weeping ones who adore and the curious ones who merely gape. He is the gentle foster father of Jesus, a rural carpenter named Joseph.

The best in him rejoices with the others. God has finally come to his people! The worst in him still wonders if he isn't the biggest fool in Bethlehem tonight.

JOURNAL: *In the celebration of Christmas, Joseph is often an overlooked figure. Why do you think he gets overlooked? What are your impressions of Joseph?*

The First to Struggle

> *Mary was pledged to be married to Joseph, but before they came together,*
> *she was found to be with child through the Holy Spirit.*
> *Because Joseph her husband was a righteous man and did not want to expose her*
> *to public disgrace, he had in mind to divorce her quietly.*
> *But after he had considered this, an angel of the Lord appeared to him in a dream and said,*
> *"Joseph son of David, do not be afraid to take Mary home as your wife,*
> *because what is conceived in her is from the Holy Spirit."*

MATTHEW 1:18-20

Joseph was the first person to really struggle with the incarnation. Mary's momentary "How could these things be?" seemed to come and go like a cool breeze. But Joseph saw no angels. He only dreamed dreams. He had no quickening in his belly to tell him that life had indeed been conceived without his flesh. We know almost nothing about Joseph, apart from his gentleness and willingness to say "No" to himself for Mary's sake and for God's.

APPLY: *Do you ever feel that you are on the sidelines of what God is doing? Consider Joseph, who had a vital place in the Christmas story yet seems to play a minor role.*

How Could It Be?

> When Joseph woke up, he did what the angel of the Lord
> had commanded him and took Mary home as his wife.
> But he had no union with her until she gave birth to a son.
> And he gave him the name Jesus.

MATTHEW 1:24-25

Imagine the dilemma of that simple man, finding himself cast in the role of father to the Son of God. Though that beautiful infant was not part of his body, the baby must have quickly taken over Joseph's heart, as most adopted children have a way of doing. As he held that squirming bundle in his arms, Joseph must have asked the question every new father asks himself and God, "How could it be?"

I first heard that question when my older brother held his son for the first time. I asked myself the same question a few years later when our first daughter, Katherine, was born. It is a question for which there is no answer. We really don't expect one. Joseph probably didn't expect an answer either.

PRAY: *Thank God for the wonders he has done which make you say, "How can this be?"*

Impossible Tasks

An angel of the Lord appeared to Joseph in a dream.
"Get up," he said, "take the child and his mother and escape to Egypt.
Stay there until I tell you, for Herod is going to search for the child to kill him."

MATTHEW 1:13

It is an impossible task, being a parent. Not just difficult . . . impossible. To take a life from its first breath on through to maturity—to feed, clothe, educate and all the rest. How could it be?

God is the giver of such impossible tasks. He says to 100-year-old Abraham and 90-year-old Sarah, "Make a baby!" He tells a young virgin, "You are with child." He informs a young, confused carpenter, who has never so much as touched his bride-to-be, "You are a father!" Perhaps in the end it's not our abilities but simply the fact that he says so. It is not a matter of what we can or cannot do but of God's power.

PRAY: *Bring all your impossibilities to God. Ask him to act according to his will.*

How Did He Do?

> *After Herod died, an angel of the Lord*
> *appeared in a dream to Joseph in Egypt and said,*
> *"Get up, take the child and his mother and go to the land of Israel,*
> *for those who were trying to take the child's life are dead."*

MATTHEW 2:19-20

So now Joseph (who is also, by the way, a virgin) is a father. His task, along with the already impossible task of fatherhood? To be a father to the Son of God!

How did Joseph do? We have no scenes of him with Jesus in the carpenter shop. But since Jesus was also known as a carpenter, he must have learned his trade from Joseph. We know that Jesus made it to manhood with a wonderfully strong and simple vision of what *father* meant. Before he shrieked "Abba!" with a man's tormented voice in Gethsemane, he must have tenderly called out that name in a child's innocent voice to that man in the shadows, Joseph.

JOURNAL: *Who are the people who influenced you as a child? What children have you influenced, or are you influencing now? How do you see God's sovereign love in your life and their lives?*

For All the People

Do not be afraid. I bring you good news of great joy that will be for all the people.
Today in the town of David a Savior has been born to you; he is Christ the Lord.
This will be a sign to you: You will find a baby wrapped in cloths and lying in a manger.

LUKE 2:10-12

Christmas tells us that we are pretty much all alike. We are, all of us, invited to come to the stable and stand together in the muck, looking to the One who has come and who promises to eventually lift us out of the muck. We are invited to worship One who was as ready to forgive and embrace an unrepentant Judas as he was a broken-hearted and ashamed Simon Peter. That is the Light that has come into the world, and those who know him need never walk in darkness again.

APPLY: *Christmas is good news for all people. Who do you know that needs to be reminded of the good news, or perhaps to hear it for the first time?*

M O N D A Y   *Silent Night?*

> But when the fullness of time had come, God sent his Son, born of a woman,
> born under the law, in order to redeem those who were under the law,
> so that we might receive adoption as children.

GALATIANS 4:4-5 NRSV

I had just finished giving a talk on the poverty of the nativity of Jesus to a group at a small country church when one sweet lady walked up to me and said, "I simply do not agree with your picture of the birth of Jesus!" I asked her why not. She replied, "I don't believe he cried the way you said." I gently pressed her for a passage from the Bible that would lead her to believe such a thing, but she couldn't come up with anything. Finally, I suppose out of desperation, she retorted, "Well, what about 'Silent Night, Holy Night'?"

That dear sister is an extreme example of our tendency to incorporate our traditions into Scripture. We sing "Away in a Manger" and believe what we sing: "No crying he makes." We thereby dismiss the examples we see every day from a multitude of newborns! I wonder if, way back in our minds, we believe he never soiled a diaper!

JOURNAL: *When you think of Jesus as a baby, do you place him in some super-human category? What do we lose by thinking of him as somehow different from any other baby?*

Sprinkles of Snow

And there were shepherds living out in the fields nearby,
keeping watch over their flocks at night.

LUKE 2:8

We celebrate the birth of Jesus in December, so we sprinkle snow on our nativity scenes and sermonize about Joseph and Mary's struggle with the cold. In truth, the Bible says nothing about the season, apart from a reference to the fact that the shepherds were "keeping watch" in the fields all through the night, which might mean it was the season when lambs were being born, the only time shepherds stay in the fields all night. If that is so, Jesus was probably born in the spring. I'd like to think it was April, since that is the month of my own birthday!

These false images of the nativity have provided the foundation for a distorted picture of Jesus' entire life, which simply must go if we are to try to grasp the real picture, given in the Gospels, of the nativity of Jesus.

PRAY: *Praise God that even though Jesus' birth was miraculous, in many ways it was very ordinary. He truly was one of us.*

W E D N E S D A Y

God's Fantastic Promise

Now there was a man in Jerusalem called Simeon, who was righteous and devout.
He was waiting for the consolation of Israel, and the Holy Spirit was upon him.
It had been revealed to him by the Holy Spirit that he would not die
before he had seen the Lord's Christ.

LUKE 2:25-26

Simeon was an old man when he received a very special promise from God, that he would not die until he had seen the coming of the Messiah. For an elderly Jew and a man of faith, there was no greater promise. From that time on, Simeon spent the remainder of his days waiting, as did all the faithful who lived before the advent of Jesus. Having faith meant waiting for God to keep his promise. Abraham. Moses. The prophets. All those who trusted God demonstrated their faith by their ability to wait. So Simeon waited in the temple for God to make good on his fantastic promise.

JOURNAL: *What are you waiting for? When do you feel most impatient? What enables you to have patience and wait for God to act?*

A Baby Wrapped in Rags

When the parents brought in the child Jesus to do
for him what the custom of the Law required,
Simeon took him in his arms and praised God.

LUKE 2:27-28

W do not know what Simeon was expecting, though we can guess. Perhaps as he sat in the temple court, he kept his eyes focused on the sky, waiting for the clouds to part and reveal a great and glorious king. Perhaps he was expecting a warrior. Many hoped the Messiah would be a warlike leader who would kill the Romans.

We do not know what Simeon expected, but we know what he got. A little baby wrapped in rags, with paupers for parents. Jesus. A most unlikely person to change the world. Yet there is hardly anyone, even an unbeliever, who could imagine what this world would be like if he had not come.

APPLY: *An unlikely baby changed the world. Today be on the lookout for God to work through unlikely people and unlikely means.*

Expect the Unexpected

> Sovereign Lord, as you have promised,
> you now dismiss your servant in peace.
> For my eyes have seen your salvation,
> which you have prepared in the sight of all people,
> a light for revelation to the Gentiles
> and for glory to your people Israel.

LUKE 2:29-32

There the Holy Baby was, cradled in his mother's arms. What must have gone through Simeon's mind when God pointed out his Promised One? Simeon was wise enough to expect the unexpected from the Lord. He went straight to Joseph and Mary. Luke gives us the wonderful detail that he took Jesus and held him in his arms. That, for me, is one of the most significant moments of the nativity narratives. In this one simple man two worlds meet. The Old Testament embraces the New. For what is the Old Testament but a collection of promises?

PRAY: *Thank God for keeping his promises, both his long-term promises in the Old Testament and his personal promises for your life.*

He Embraces Us

I give them eternal life, and they shall never perish;
no one can snatch them out of my hand.

JOHN 10:28

It was good news for Simeon to finally be able to embrace the Promised One. But far and away the best news of all is that Jesus embraces us. That was the reason for his coming. Most of us describe our coming to faith by saying, "I've asked Jesus into my life." We should really say he has invited us into his life!

That was the reason for Simeon's song. Deep inside his tired old heart, he knew that the infant he held in his arms was in truth the One who had been holding him all his life long.

JOURNAL: *What does it mean for you that Jesus has invited you into his life?*

MONDAY *The Conquering Lamb*

> Then I saw a Lamb, looking as if it had been slain,
> standing in the center of the throne,
> encircled by the four living creatures and the elders.

REVELATION 5:6

In the Old Testament, the lamb is the helpless innocent substitute and sacrifice. He is victim, not victor. Even in the New Testament, when the Lamb of God appears he seems an unlikely conqueror. It is not until the close of the New Testament, in the book of Revelation, that the Conquering Lamb appears.

Christmas, the celebration of the first coming of the Lamb, looks back to the humble stable and the simple shepherds. The setting is a dark, fallen world. He has come to expose through his weakness the impotence of what the world calls power.

In that sense Christmas is a preparation for the celebration that will be the second coming of the Lamb triumphant. The contrast between the two settings could not be more extreme. Instead of a silent stable and bunch of motley shepherds, there will be a resplendent multitude whose praise can only be described as a *roar!*

JOURNAL: *Reflect on how the Lamb of God can be both sacrifice and conqueror. Thank him that you participate in both his humble sacrifice and his ultimate victory.*

The Moment of the Unveiling

Do not be afraid. I am the First and the Last. I am the Living One;
I was dead, and behold I am alive forever and ever!
And I hold the keys of death and Hades.

REVELATION 1:17-18

John wrote the book of Revelation to comfort believers who were looking persecution squarely in the face. He also writes to us today, who are squarely looking at the death of Christendom. Understanding his purpose in writing is not a matter of decoding or solving some complex mystery as much as it is a matter of simply listening to the Spirit. As with all Scripture, the purpose is to turn a reading eye into a listening ear.

I am drawn again and again to a single moment that John tells and retells from different angles. I would call it the moment of the Unveiling. It is the moment when Jesus is revealed, the moment he appears in the clouds, the instant he comes pounding toward us astride the white warhorse, the very "twinkling of an eye" when we see him crowned with many crowns. But more specifically for me it is the split second of realization that the Return is actually happening, the instant when you and I look up and see the reality of the Coming of Christ.

APPLY: *How often do you consider that Christ could come this very day? When are you most likely to forget about it? When are you most aware of the possibility?*

Where Will You Be?

Look, he is coming with the clouds,
and every eye will see him,
even those who pierced him;
and all the peoples of the earth will mourn because of him.
So shall it be! Amen.

REVELATION 1:7

Where will you be? What will you be doing? Will you hear the sound of the trumpet and look out your office window? "Did you hear something?" you will ask someone sitting next to you.

Imagine for a moment what you will see. What will it feel like to realize fully what is happening to you and the rest of the world? "So, it has all been true after all!" John wants us to savor that split second. That moment will not be wasted in deciphering. (*Oh, the locusts aren't B-52s!*) It will be a moment when the Bible says Jesus—not the signs—will be "marveled at by those who believe." The moment when all we ever hoped for will be unveiled and we shall see him at last!

PRAY: *Thank the Lord for the certainty of his return. Pray that he will find you faithfully doing the work he has given you.*

Worship with the Saints

After this I looked, and there before me was a door standing open in heaven.

REVELATION 4:1

For the biblical prophets, a transport into the heavenlies was an experience over which they had little or no control, apart from their own obedient willingness to be God's people at that time, in that place.

Today, for us, God provides another means by which we cover the distance: the vehicle of worship, which can transport us to that miraculous heavenly place. We too can take our place alongside the multitude and sing the same songs. We can, in faith, be present at the very throne of God.

If you are rolling your eyes at this notion and thinking, *I see no throne when I worship,* you misunderstand the real purpose of worship. It is not to provide us with an experience. Regardless of whether we might be aware of our presence alongside the heavenly multitude, faith tells us we are in fact together with them, bonded by worship, giving our praise to God. Your shouts and songs and words of worship are heard by the same God in the same throne room, and in precisely the same place—beyond time! Whenever we truly worship, we worship with the saints.

APPLY: *What do you think of as the purpose of worship? How does your viewpoint change as you think of yourself and your fellow worshipers on earth joined with the worshipers in heaven?*

Worthy Is the Lamb!

Worthy is the Lamb, who was slain,
to receive power and wealth and wisdom and strength
and honor and glory and praise!

REVELATION 5:12

Doesn't all real joy, even the joy of heaven—perhaps especially the joy of heaven—contain at its heart a twinge, a bit of black cloth against which the diamond of joy seems especially beautiful? When we stand at last before the Lamb, who will still bear his healing wounds, will we not, amidst the inexpressible joy, think back to his suffering, to the suffering of our tired old world, or even to our own suffering?

"You are the Lamb that was slain!" will be our shout, our word of praise. You, our blessed, meek, glorious Servant, suffered for this moment! And so we will surely glory over his woundedness and perhaps weep because of it. But compared to the joy, the tears will seem as a drop in the great blue ocean of God's eternal joy; and those tears (if indeed there are tears) will be gently wiped away.

JOURNAL: *How would your image of Jesus be lessened if he had never suffered?*

"Oh Lord, Come!"

He who testifies to these things says, "Yes, I am coming soon."
Amen. Come, Lord Jesus.

REVELATION 22:20

The yearning to see Jesus is spelled out in the heart cry *Maranatha!* It's an Aramaic word that means "Oh Lord, come!" The early Christians actually believed that the word *maranatha* would hasten the Lord's return.

Jesus leaves us, not with secret signs that only spiritual giants can discern. No, he leaves simple and easy-to-understand instructions to his beloved children. What we're left with is not concrete pronouncements about events. He gives us words of simplicity that force us to rely on him. We must preach the gospel to all nations, not analyze the numerical value of the name of a world leader. He himself will let us know when he has returned, for we shall all see him, and absolutely no one knows the hour. Jesus leaves us with a future hope that, by faith, transforms our present reality with him.

So what we are left with is faith, hope and a special word that might very well hasten his coming after all, *Maranatha!* Oh Lord, come!

PRAY: *Pray "Oh Lord, come! And let me help others to be ready for your return."*

Material in this devotional is drawn from various writings of Michael Card, including the following books:

A Fragile Stone: The Emotional Life of Simon Peter. Downers Grove, Ill.: InterVarsity Press, 2003.

Immanuel: Reflections on the Life of Christ. Nashville: Thomas Nelson, 1990.

The Promise. Nashville: Sparrow, 1991.

Scribbling in the Sand: Christ and Creativity. Downers Grove, Ill.: InterVarsity Press, 2002.

Unveiled Hope (with Scotty Smith). Nashville: Thomas Nelson, 1997.